PAINLESS

French

Carol Chaitkin, M.S.

Lynn Gore, M.A.

Third Edition

About the Authors

Carol Chaitkin is a graduate of Pomona College, the University of California at Berkeley, and Cornell University. She has also studied at the Sorbonne and at the Institut de Phonétique in Paris. She spent most of her career as a high school English teacher and department head in the Great Neck, New York, public schools. Following her retirement from Great Neck in 1999, she was appointed *proviseure adjointe* and director of American Studies at the Lycée Français de New York, where she served until 2003. Chaitkin is also the author of Barron's *Let's Review: English* and of *Regents Examinations and Answers: English*. She hopes *Painless French* will lead readers to share her admiration for the logic, richness, and beauty of the French language.

Lynn Gore, a retired French teacher, received her B.A. in French from Hartwick College in Oneonta, New York, and her M.A. in French Literature from the University of Wisconsin, Madison. She taught all levels of French in New York's Mid-Hudson Valley, and led over thirty trips to francophone countries with her former French Club. She served as president on two occasions for ALOUD—the Association of Language teachers of Orange, Ulster and Duchess Counties—and as a regional director and secretary for NYSAFLT (New York State Association of Foreign Language Teachers). She feels that grammar has and always will be the foundation of strong language acquisition, but believes that it should be as "painless" as possible by emphasizing strong communication skills and cultural insights. Her goal as a teacher is for students to learn life skills and compassion for others through learning a foreign language.

Acknowledgments

The authors would like to thank the following for excerpts that appear in this book. Every effort has been made to track down the copyright holders, and we apologize in advance for any unintended omissions. We would be pleased to insert the appropriate acknowledgments in any subsequent edition of this publication.

Chapter 3: *L'île lointaine*, by Daniel Thaly. Adapted from http://www.vertpomme.net.
Chapter 4: *Les Morts ne sont pas Morts*, by Birago Diop. Adapted from *Birago Diop, Les contes d'Amadou Koumba*, Editions Présence Africaine, Dakar, 1961.
Chapter 6: *Les Champs-Elysées*, words and music by Pierre Delanoé. Adapted from www.paroles.net.
Chapter 11: *Les Gouverneurs de la Rosée*, by Jacques Roumain. Adapted from *Littérature moderne du monde francophone—une anthologie*, by Peter S. Thompson, National Textbook Co., 1997.
Chapter 12: *Le Petit Prince*, by Antoine de Saint-Exupéry. Adapted from Editions Gallimard, Paris, 1946.
Chapter 12: *Ma Louisianne*, lyrics by Zachary Richard. Adapted from *Littérature moderne du monde francophone—une anthologie*, by Peter S. Thompson, National Textbook Co., 1997.

All inquiries should be addressed to:
Barron's Educational Series, Inc.
250 Wireless Boulevard
Hauppauge, New York 11788
www.barronseduc.com

ISBN: 978-1-4380-0770-0

Library of Congress Control No. 2015947872

PRINTED IN CANADA
9 8 7 6 5 4 3 2 1

CONTENTS

Chapitre 4: Ce que j'aime faire: Nos activitiés (What I like to do: Activities)　71

Chapitre 5: Ce que j'aime manger: La nourriture (What I like to eat: Meals and food)　97

INTRODUCTION

Painless French offers an introduction to French vocabulary, grammar, literature, and culture for students as early as those in middle school, but welcomes readers of any age. The underlying approach is "In English we say this . . . and in French we say this . . ." Featuring a variety of brief sections, illustrated in a manner characteristic of the "Painless" series, the chapters are organized thematically and are introduced by Sophie, a young French girl who lives with her family in Paris. The essential elements of French grammar are presented *in comparison with* the relevant elements of English grammar, with differences and similarities highlighted in the *Vive la différence!* and *Attention!* sections.

Although you may approach this book in any order, the presentation of grammatical elements is progressively complex from chapter to chapter and often makes reference to prior sections or chapters; these are regularly followed by brief exercises—Brain Ticklers—asking you to apply what has just been introduced or illustrated. On the other hand, each chapter in *Painless French* offers extensive lists of vocabulary and idioms related to the overall theme, which may be explored at any time you find yourself asking "I wonder what the French word for . . . is? (*Comment dit-on?*)" You will also find examples of what are called *amis* and *faux amis*—"friends" and "false friends." These are words identical or similar in spelling in French and English. While the *amis* (cognates) have similar or identical meanings, the *faux amis* (false cognates) are words whose meanings are different in the two languages. If you are interested in how common proverbs are expressed in the two languages, look for the young man in the beret and *Proverbe: Didier dit!*

Among the most important features of *Painless French* are the numerous passages in English, offering background in French history and culture, which include interesting contrasts with American experience. These may be highlighted as *Info*, *Tu sais quoi?*, or *C'est intéressant.* Topics range from aspects of French history to features of modern society, from the natural world to modern technology; and they include such universal subjects as education, sports and leisure, and the arts. You will even find a brief explanation of how and why the *restaurant* was invented in France!

French is an official language in more than 30 countries on five continents, and along with English, it is the only language to be spoken or taught in nearly every country of the world. Several chapters include a poem or song representing one of the many different francophone cultures, and Sophie or her friends send *cartes postales* (post cards) from places of interest within France and abroad, including Québec, Africa, and the Caribbean. *Painless French* is written to help you become part of this world.

Carol Chaitkin
Lynn Gore

Me voilà!

HERE I AM—SOPHIE

Bonjour! Ça va? Je m'appelle Sophie. Je vais bien. J'ai treize ans et j'habite à Paris, alors je suis française. Je suis brune et de taille moyenne. J'ai les yeux bruns et les cheveux châtain clair. Mes amis me disent que je suis assez mignonne et sympa, mais mes parents pensent que je suis un peu paresseuse mais très intelligente. J'assiste au collège où je suis en cinquième.

Vocabulaire

bonjour	hello
salut	hi
je m'appelle	my name is
j'ai treize ans	I'm thirteen years old
j'ai les yeux bruns	I have brown eyes
bleus	blue
les cheveux châtain clair	light brown hair
blonds	blond
je suis	I am
je ne suis pas	I am not
un peu	a little
assez	rather
très	very
trop	too
sympa	nice
laid/e	ugly
méchant/e	mean
mignon/ne	cute
paresseux/euse	lazy
petit/e	little/short

de taille moyenne	average size
grand/e	tall
à l'école	in elementary school
au collège	in middle school
au lycée	in high school

ATTENTION!

Adjectives describe masculine or feminine objects or people. The extra letters are used to describe females, so Sophie is *mignonne* (feminine), but her dog Max is *mignon*. Adjectives are also singular or plural in agreement with the nouns they modify or describe. *Tu as les yeux verts.* You have green eyes. Green, *verts*, has an s to agree with the plural eyes, *les yeux*. You will learn more about adjectives in the next chapter.

BRAIN TICKLERS
Set # 1

Exercises (This word is almost the same as English. Pronounce it with emphasis on the last syllable: "eggs er ceese.")

A. Fill in the blanks with the French words from the vocabulary list to describe Sophie.

1. Je _____ m'appelle _____ Sophie.
   (My name is Sophie.)

2. J'ai _TREiZE Ams_ .
(I'm thirteen years old.)

3. Je suis _de Taille moyenne_ .
(I am average size.)

4. J'ai les _yeux brums_ .
(I have brown eyes.)

5. Je suis _____ .
(I am French.)

B. How do you say the following in French?

1. Hello _bom four_

2. I am _Je suis_

3. a little _petiT_

4. lazy _euse_

5. in middle school _au collège_

C. Talk about yourself. Answer these questions in French:

1. What is your name?

2. What is your nationality?

3. Are you tall?

(Answers are on page 20.)

Vocabulaire	
Quelques nationalités	**Some Nationalities**
africain/e	African
américain/e	American
anglais/e	English
canadien/ne	Canadian
chinois/e	Chinese
espagnol/e	Spanish
français/e	French

mexicain/e	Mexican
indien/ne	Indian
irlandais/e	Irish
italien/ne	Italian
japonais/e	Japanese

Vive la différence!

In English and in French, we capitalize geographical names (countries, states, cities, towns, etc.)—New York, Paris, Bordeaux, Provence, France, United States—*mais* (but) you will see that some rules for capitalization are different in French. When talking about nationalities in general, there is no capitalization, yet if you refer to a specific person you would say *un Francais*, a Frenchman, or *un Américain*, an American, *mais* (but)

Sophie est française.	Sophie is French.
Robert est américain.	Robert is American.
Mon cousin est canadien.	My cousin is Canadian.
Le drapeau français	the French flag
Le drapeau américain	the American flag

Encore une différence!

In English we capitalize the names of languages and their adjective forms; in French we do *not* capitalize the names of languages and their adjective forms:

Jacques parle français en France, mais il parle anglais aux Etats-Unis.

(James speaks French in France, but he speaks English in the United States.)

C'est curieux!

Did you notice? In the preceding French phrases, the adjectives *français and américain* **follow the noun** *drapeau;* in the

English phrases, the adjectives French and American **precede the noun** flag. We will study formation and placement of adjectives in greater detail later, but for now note the following general principle: If the adjective is used literally, it follows the noun; if it is used in a more figurative way, it usually precedes.

Répète après moi!

Why does the French language sound so different from English? The main reason is that the vowels are pronounced differently. Start by practicing the basic sounds and learn the vowels well. When you learn the rules you will see that it is easy.

a (ah)	*y* (ee)
e (euh)	*o* (oh)
i (ee)	*u* (uy)

H is silent, so if you try a simple English word with a French accent like "Ohio," it is pronounced "oh ee oh." You're on your way!

Here are few more common vowel sounds and their pronunciation in French:

ais	(ay) (the final -s is not pronounced)
au, eau	(oh)
oi	(wah)
ou, où	(oo)
uis	(wee)

What about accents? Many words in French have accents. These are part of the **spelling** of the words and may also indicate a specific sound. For example, the letter é is pronounced -ay, but the letter è is pronounced -eh.

Here are the consonants and vowels again. Practice them until you can "sing" the alphabet song in French:

A (ah) B (bé) C (cé) D (dé) . . .
E (euh) F (effe) G (gé) . . .
H (hache) I (ee) J (jee) K (ka) . . .
L (elle) M (emme) N (enne) O (oh) P (pé) . . .

Q (ku) R (erre) S (esse) . . .
T (té) U (u) V (vé) . . .
W (double vé) X (ixe) Y (i grec) Z (zède)

Grammaire

If you want to talk about other people, you will need to know how to conjugate verbs. *Je suis* (I am) comes from the verb *être*, and *j'ai* (I have) comes from the verb *avoir*. First look at the subject pronouns:

Je	(I)	*Nous*	(we)
Tu	(you)	*Vous*	(you)
Il	(he)	*Ils*	(they)
Elle	(she)	*Elles*	(they—all feminine)

ATTENTION!

You may have noticed there are two ways of saying *you* on the list: **tu** and **vous**. In old English, the words *thou* and *thy* were used to mean *you* in a polite or formal situation. Although we no longer say thou in English, **vous** is used in modern French for addressing an adult or someone you would address as Mr. or Mrs., like your doctor, a neighbor, or the teacher. **Vous** is also used for the plural, for example when you are talking to a few friends. **Tu** is used to mean *you* when you are talking to one friend, family member, small child, or pet. **Vous** is formal or plural, and **tu** is familiar.

Here are conjugations of the verbs *être* (to be) and *avoir* (to have):

Etre		*Avoir*	
Je suis	I am	*J'ai*	I have
Tu es	You are	*Tu as*	You have
Il est	He is	*Il a*	He has
Elle est	She is	*Elle a*	She has
Nous sommes	We are	*Nous avons*	We have
Vous êtes	You are	*Vous avez*	You have
Ils sont	They are	*Ils ont*	They have
Elles sont	They are	*Elles ont*	They have

BRAIN TICKLERS
Set # 2

A. *Tu or vous*? How would you address the following people?
   1. your mother *tu*
   2. your school principal *vous*
   3. your dentist *tu*
   4. your best friend *tu*
   5. two cousins *tu*

B. How would you write the forms of *avoir* in these exercises? As you fill in the blanks, think about what each sentence means and say it out loud.

1. *Tu __Ai__ les yeux bleus.*
2. *Nous __Ai__ treize ans.*
3. *Vous _____ les cheveux châtain clair.*
4. *Mes parents _____ quarante (40) ans.* (use the *ils* form)
5. *Sophie _____ les yeux bleus.* (use the *elle* form)

C. How would you write the forms of *être* in these exercises?
   1. *Marc _____ sympa.*
   2. *Nous _____ intelligents.*
   3. *Tu _____ petit.*

(Answers are on page 20.)

Vive la différence!

In this section we contrast French and English to help you appreciate the interesting similarities and differences between the two languages.

When you express your age in French, you use the verb *avoir*, to have, so you are literally saying how many years you have: *J'ai treize ans*, I have thirteen years. Don't forget to include the word *ans* even though in English you can say "I'm thirteen." Of course when you translate this into English, you say "I am thirteen."

Vocabulaire: Encore c'est mieux

Numbers

Start to memorize the numbers in French. Try grouping the lower numbers by threes and tap as you say them to establish a rhythm:

1-Un 2-deux 3-trois
(tap tap tap)

4-quatre 5-cinq 6-six
(tap tap tap)

7-sept 8-huit 9-neuf
(tap tap tap)

10-dix
(bang with two hands)

11-onze 12-douze 13-treize
(tap tap tap)

14-quatorze 15-quinze 16-seize
(tap-tap tap tap)

17-dix-sept 18-dix-huit 19-dix-neuf
(tap-tap tap-tap tap-tap)

20-vingt
(bang with two hands)

The higher numbers are created by adding 1 to 9 as in English. Note that 60 to 79 and 80 to 99 are formed by adding 1 to 19.

21 vingt et un (numbers 21, 31, 41, 51, 61, and 71 use the word et)

22 vingt-deux (other numbers under 100 use hyphens)

23 vingt-trois

30 trente

40 quarante

50 cinquante

60 soixante

70 soixante-dix

75 soixante-quinze

80 quatre-vingts

81 quatre-vingt-un

90 quatre-vingt-dix

94 quatre-vingt quatorze

100 cent

BRAIN TICKLERS
Set # 3

Unscramble the words to find these numbers: 71, 35, 42, 14, 6.

1. ixs
2. zeqtauor
3. tequaran-xeud
4. retten-qcin
5. xasteoin-zneo-et

(Answers are on page 20.)

Vocabulaire

Here are some more adjectives:

aimable	friendly
chic	chic (cool, sophisticated)
dynamique	dynamic
mystérieux/mystérieuse	mysterious
optimiste	optimistic
pessimiste	pessimistic
poli/e	polite
réaliste	realistic
religieux/religieuse	religious
sérieux/sérieuse	serious
sincère	sincere
sportif/sportive	athletic
timide	shy

BRAIN TICKLERS
Set # 4

Using the correct form of être, to be, say the following in French:

1. He is polite.

2. She is serious.

3. I am optimistic.

4. You (sing. fam.) are friendly.

5. We are athletic.

(Answers are on page 20.)

 **Vive la différence!**

In French, we also use the verb *avoir* to describe people and how they feel.

Note the following expressions using the verb *avoir*:

avoir chaud	to be warm
avoir froid	to be cold
avoir treize ans	to be thirteen years old
avoir sommeil	to be sleepy
avoir faim	to be hungry
avoir soif	to be thirsty
avoir peur	to be afraid
avoir raison	to be right
avoir tort	to be wrong, mistaken

For example, to say:

I am thirteen years old.	*J'ai treize ans.* (lit. I have thirteen years)
You (fam.) are cold.	*Tu as froid.*
She is right.	*Elle a raison.*
We are thirsty.	*Nous avons soif.*
They are hungry.	*Ils ont faim.*

BRAIN TICKLERS
Set # 5

Practice using avoir *to compose the following expressions:*

1. He is afraid.

2. She is thirsty.

3. I am cold.

4. They are right.

5. You (pl.) are warm.

6. We are hungry.

7. She is fourteen years old.

8. He is sleepy.

(Answers are on page 20.)

Vocabulaire

Parts of the Body

le corps	body
la poitrine	chest
le dos	back
la tête	head
le cou	neck
la figure	face
le bras	arm
la main	hand
les doigts	fingers
la jambe	leg
le genou	knee
le pied	foot

Proverbe: Didier dit

Loin des yeux, loin du coeur
Out of sight, out of mind
(Literally: Far from the eyes, far from the heart)

Répète après moi!

In this section you will learn more about perfecting a good French accent. Of course you'll need to listen to French speakers. Try to meet other students or people who speak French to help you. The Internet has radio and television stations online in French. Good places to start are *www.franceinter.fr* and *www.rfi.fr*. Look for *écouter* or *écoutez* to find items you can listen to. There are also many free or inexpensive apps for smartphones and tablets.

One basic difference between French and English is that the final consonant is generally silent. For example, the word *bras* (arm) is pronounced "bra." There are some exceptions (*bien sûr*) (of course). Be <u>careful</u> and watch for words that end in crfl (careful). Pronounce the final consonants in the following words: *chi<u>c</u>, ca<u>r</u>, sporti<u>f</u>, be<u>l</u>*.

When an e follows a consonant, then that consonant is pronounced: for example, *optimis<u>t</u>e, mystérieu<u>s</u>e, tê<u>t</u>e*.

Final vowels are also pronounced: *fada* (nuts, crazy), *poli* (polite), *radio, perdu* (lost), *coucou* (here I am).

Also remember to put more emphasis on the final syllable of a French word:

English	French
radio	*ra<u>dio</u>*
accent	*ac<u>cent</u>*
photo	*pho<u>to</u>*

Vocabulaire

More Expressions Using *être* and *avoir*

There are many ways to talk to people about how they are feeling. If you are talking to a friend, you will use different expressions than when you are talking to an adult or a stranger.

To a friend	To an adult
Ça va? How's it going?	
Comment vas-tu? How are you?	*Comment allez-vous?* How are you?
Ça va bien. It's going well.	*Je vais bien.* I feel well.
Ça va très bien. It's going very well.	*Je vais très bien.* I feel very well.
Ça va comme ci commeça.	*Je vais comme ci commeça.* (so so)
Ça va mal. It's going badly.	*Je vais mal.* I feel bad.
Qu'est-ce que tu as? or *Qu'as-tu?* What's wrong?	*Qu'est-ce que vous avez?* What's wrong?
Où as-tu mal? Where does it hurt?	*Où avez-vous mal?* Where does it hurt?

Use the verb *être* to say whether you are healthy or sick:

Je suis malade.	I am sick.
Je suis enrhumé.	I have a cold.
Je suis en bonne santê.	I am healthy (in good health).

We use *avoir mal à* to name a specific pain or illness:

avoir mal à la tête	to have a headache
avoir mal à la gorge	to have a sore throat
avoir mal aux dents	to have a toothache
avoir mal au dos	to have a backache
avoir mal au pied	to have pain in the foot
avoir mal aux mains	to have pain in the hands

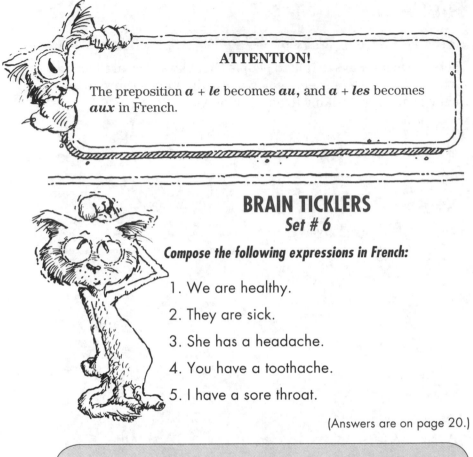

ATTENTION!

The preposition *a* + *le* becomes *au*, and *a* + *les* becomes *aux* in French.

BRAIN TICKLERS
Set # 6

Compose the following expressions in French:

1. We are healthy.

2. They are sick.

3. She has a headache.

4. You have a toothache.

5. I have a sore throat.

(Answers are on page 20.)

A réfléchir

The French language is a Romance language similar to the other Romance languages derived from Latin, the language of the Romans. The principal romance languages are Italian, Spanish, French, Romanian, and Portuguese. Julius Caesar, seeking to expand his empire, landed in Provence in southern France in 54 BC and brought the language of the Romans to Gaul, which was France's former name. Besides building an efficient transportation network of roads, the Romans built impressive monuments like giant aqueducts, arenas, and theaters, the likes of which the Gauls had never

seen before. The Roman soldiers taught the Gauls their language, and the resulting combinations of the two languages evolved into French. Once you learn French you will be able to learn the other Romance languages more easily, although each one is quite different. Nouns in Romance languages are either masculine or feminine. We'll learn more about that in Chapter 2. You will also see that many French words look nearly the same in English. These are called *cognates.* This is because William the Conqueror of France brought the French language to England in 1066 when he invaded England. French remained the official language of England for over a century. The English language acquired terms from the French language that are still used today for fashion, cuisine, society, literature, and politics—like a *coup d'état*—government overthrow. *Bon uppélit,* enjoy your meal, and *faux pas,* social blunder, are other examples. Up to 40 percent of the English language has words of French origin!

BRAIN TICKLERS
Set # 7

Answer these questions about the French language:

1. Name three Romance languages.

2. Who invaded France in 54 BC?

3. What did the Romans build in France?

4. Who brought the French language to England?

5. What are cognates?

(Answers are on page 20.)

Amis/Faux Amis

As you learned, the English language developed with significant influences and elements from French, and because both languages developed in part from Latin, there are many cognates, or words in the two languages that have the same origins. These words have similar spellings and meanings. This means you have already recognized many familiar words in French. Here are a few more examples of some common words in French and their English cognates:

aventure	adventure
curieux	curious
conséquence	consequence
décider	decide
difficile	difficult
lettre	letter
médecine	medicine
objet	object
personnel	personal
retour	return
sujet	subject
tourner	to turn (verb)

But there are many false cognates, or *faux amis* (false friends); these are words or expressions that have similar spellings (and origins) but over time have developed very different meanings in the two languages. Here are a few notorious examples:

achever (v) to finish or complete something; it does not mean "to achieve."

actuel (adj.) at this moment; it does not mean "actual."

assister (v) to help or assist; but it also means "to attend" or "to be present."

bureau (nm) desk or office; in French, it is not the dresser where you put your clothes.

collège (nm) middle school (grades 6 through 9 in France); it does not refer to college or university.

confuse (adj.) embarrassed; it does not mean "confused."

correct (adj.) appropriate, polite, honest; not generally used to mean "right answer."

déception (nf) disappointment; it does not mean "deception."

éditeur (nm) publisher; it does not mean "editor."

figure (nf) face; not used to mean numbers or one's "shape"!

football (nm) English word used in French for the game of soccer, not U.S. football.

grand (adj.) tall, to describe people

lecture (nf) means reading; it does not mean "lecture" as in English.

librairie (nf) bookstore; in French, the word for library is *bibliothèque.*

roman (nm) a novel; in French, the word for Roman is spelled *romain.*

sale (adj.) dirty, soiled; the French word for sale is *soldes,* and *à vendre* means for sale.

sensible (adj.) sensitive; in French, a sensible person is described as *raisonnable.*

Misusing these words can lead you to say or write something awkward and even embarrassing. Throughout *Painless French,* you will find examples of *amis* and *faux amis.*

BRAIN TICKLERS—THE ANSWERS

Set # 1, page 4
A.
1. *m'appelle*
2. *treize ans*
3. *de taille moyenne*
4. *yeux bruns*
5. *française*

B.
1. *bonjour*
2. *je suis*
3. *un peu*
4. *paresseux/paresseuse*
5. *au collège*

C.
Answers will vary.

Set # 2, page 9
A.
1. *tu*
2. *vous*
3. *vous*
4. *tu*
5. *vous*

B.
1. *as*
2. *avons*
3. *avez*
4. *ont*
5. *a*

C.
1. *est*
2. *sommes*
3. *es*

Set # 3, page 11
1. *six*
2. *quatorze*
3. *quarante-deux*
4. *trente-cinq*
5. *soixante et onze*

Set # 4, page 12
1. *Il est poli.*
2. *Elle est sérieuse.*
3. *Je suis optimiste.*
4. *Tu es aimable.*
5. *Nous sommes sportifs/ sportives.*

Set # 5, page 13
1. *Il a peur.*
2. *Elle a soif.*
3. *J'ai froid.*
4. *Ils/Elles ont raison.*
5. *Vous avez chaud.*
6. *Nous avons faim.*
7. *Elle a quatorze ans.*
8. *Il a sommeil.*

Set # 6, page 16
1. *Nous sommes en bonne santé.*
2. *Ils/Elles sont malades.*
3. *Elle a mal à la tête.*
4. *Vous avez mal aux dents.*
5. *J'ai mal à la gorge.*

Set # 7, page 17
1. French, Italian, Spanish, Romanian, or Portuguese are choices.
2. Julius Caesar
3. road system, monuments, arenas, theaters, etc.
4. William the Conqueror
5. Words that appear to be the same or very similar

Voici ma famille, mes amis, mes voisins

MEET MY FAMILY, FRIENDS, AND NEIGHBORS

Salut! C'est Sophie. Ça va? Je voudrais présenter ma famille.
Nous avons une petite famille aimable. Mon père s'appelle
Bertrand et ma mère s'appelle Hélène. Ils ont trente-huit ans tous
les deux et ils sont gentils, mais un peu sévères. J'ai un frère,
Jean-Luc, qui a seize ans. Il est intelligent mais parfois pénible!
Mes grands-parents habitent dans la banlieue (suburb) de Paris,
pas très loin de chez nous. La sœur de mon père est ma tante
Françoise. C'est une jeune femme superbe qui habite à Nice
au sud de la France. Elle a vingt-huit ans et j'adore lui rendre
visite. Ma meilleure copine s'appelle Lucie. C'est une petite
fille formidable—elle est toujours optimiste et amusante! J'ai
un petit chien Max. C'est un teckel (dachsund) qui est curieux
et très actif. Nous avons aussi un vieux chat paresseux qui
s'appelle Filou. Nos voisins, les Leblanc, sont de bons amis avec
mes parents. Ils ont deux filles jumelles de quatre ans, Marie et
Chantal. De temps en temps je fais du baby-sitting chez eux.

Vocabulaire

La famille   Family

la femme woman/wife	*l'homme* (man) *le mari* (husband)
la mère mother	*le père* father
la belle-mère stepmother	*le beau-père* stepfather
la belle-fille stepdaughter	*le beau-fils* stepson
la belle-sœur stepsister	*le beau-frère* stepbrother
la sœur sister	*le frère* brother
les parents parents	*les grands-parents* grandparents
la grand-mère grandmother	*le grand-père* grandfather
la fille daughter/girl	*le fils* son *le garçon* boy
la tante aunt	*l'oncle* uncle
la nièce niece	*le neveu* nephew

la jumelle twin (girl)	*le jumeau* twin (boy)
la cousine cousin (girl)	*le cousin* cousin (boy)

Les amis   Friends

l'amie friend (girl)	*l'ami* friend (boy)
la copine close friend (girl)	*le copain* close friend (boy)
la camarade de classe	*le camarade de classe*
classmate (girl)	classmate (boy)
la voisine neighbor (female)	*le voisin* neighbor (male)

Les bêtes   Pets

le chien dog	*le chat* cat
l'oiseau bird	*le poisson rouge* goldfish
le hamster hamster	*le cochon d'inde* guinea pig

Miscellanées   Miscellaneous

un peu a little	*le/la meilleur/e* best
s'appelle is called	*petit/e* short, small
de temps en temps sometimes	*grand/e* tall, large
la banlieue suburb	*vieux/vieille* old
bon/bonne good	*jeune* young

Grammaire
Forms Classified by Gender in French

Why is there a *la* or *le* before the nouns in the vocabulary list?

In French, nouns have gender; that is, they are classified as either masculine or feminine, and in learning vocabulary, we must learn the gender as part of the noun itself. In dictionaries and in *Painless French*, nouns are identified as *nf* (noun, feminine gender) or *nm* (noun, masculine gender). The definite article (the) has masculine or feminine forms accordingly:

la (f.) *le* (m.) = the

When you practice saying or writing your vocabulary lists, remember to include the **la** or **le** with the noun. And don't worry about occasional mistakes. The French make them too! Here are some examples of nouns from the preceding vocabulary list where the gender is directly related to the meaning and easy to remember:

la femme (nf) = woman, wife	*le mari* (nm) = husband,
	l'homme (nm) = man
la fille (nf) = girl, daughter	*le fils* (nm) = son
	le garçon (nm) = boy
la sœur (nf) = sister	*le frère* (nm) = brother
la mère (nf) = mother	*le père* (nm) = father
la tante (nf) = aunt	*l'oncle* (nm) = uncle

ATTENTION!

The definite articles **le** and **la** become **l'** when the noun—masculine or feminine—begins with a vowel or a "silent h."

Example: *l'oncle*   *l'homme*   *l'amie*

BRAIN TICKLERS
Set # 8

Write the correct form of the definite article, le, la, l', for each of the following:

1. _____garçon
2. _____beau-frère
3. _____sœur
4. _____fille
5. _____oncle

6. _____amie
7. _____fils
8. _____cousine
9. _____femme
10. _____voisin

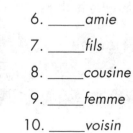

(Answers are on page 41.)

Grammaire

In French, the indefinite articles *a, an, one* **also have masculine or feminine forms:**

> *un* = a, an, one before a masculine noun: *un homme, un fils, un copain*
>
> *une* = a, an, one before a feminine noun: *une femme, une fille, une copine*

So far we have practiced with nouns and pronouns in their singular forms only. How do we make these expressions plural? As in English, the simple addition of an **-s** creates the plural form of most nouns. Here are the plural forms of some of the nouns from the preceding list:

Feminine	**Masculine**
les femmes	*les hommes*
les filles	*les garçons*
les cousines	*les cousins*
des amies	*des amis*
des sœurs	*des frères*

Note that the plural form of the articles *le, la,* or *l'* is always *les,* and the plural form of *un* or *une* is always *des.*

Definite Articles

Singular			Plural		
le	le garçon	the boy	**les**	les garçons	the boys
la	la fille	the girl	**les**	les filles	the girls
l'	l'homme	the man	**les**	les hommes	the men

Indefinite Articles

Singular			Plural		
un	un garçon	a, one boy	**des**	des garçons	(some) boys
une	une fille	a, one girl	**des**	des filles	(some) girls

Vocabulaire

Here are some additional nouns, naming familiar objects or places, to give you practice writing phrases based on what you have learned so far:

le stylo (nm)	the pen	les stylos	the pens
le cahier (nm)	the notebook	les cahiers	the notebooks
la tablette (nf)	the tablet	les tablettes	the tablets
un livre (nm)	a book	des livres	some books
un portable (nm)	a cell phone	des portables	some cell phones
une école (nf)	a school	des écoles	some schools

BRAIN TICKLERS
Set # 9

Using le, la, l', les or un, une, des, write the following expressions:

1. a tablet _____
2. the books _____
3. the school _____
4. some notebooks _____
5. a cell phone _____
6. a classroom _____
7. some tablets _____
8. one pen _____
9. the schools _____
10. the cell phone _____

(Answers are on page 41.)

Grammaire
Possessive Adjective Forms

How do we say **my brother, my sister, my father, my mother**
using the possessive adjective forms *mon* (m.) and *ma* (f.) ?

> *Mon frère*   *ma sœur*   *mon père*   *ma mère*

How do we say **my cousin, my neighbor**?

> *Mon cousin,* or *ma cousine*
> *Mon voisin,* or *ma voisine*

mais (but)

> *son frère* = his brother **or** her brother
> *sa sœur* = his sister **or** her sister

 **Vive la différence!**

The possessive adjectives agree with the object, person, or
animal that follows—that is, with what is possessed, not with
the "owner," or possessor, as in English.

Using some of the nouns you already know, this chart shows
how the plural forms of the possessive adjectives are spelled.

English	French			Examples
	masc.	fem.	plural	
my	mon	ma		*mon stylo, ma chaise* my pen, my chair
			mes	*mes stylos, mes chaises* my pens, my chairs
your	ton	ta		*ton cahier, ta sœur* your notebook, your sister
			tes	*tes cahiers, tes sœurs* your notebooks, your sisters

his/her/its	son	sa		son frère, sa sœur his/her brother, his/her sister
			ses	ses frères, ses sœurs his/her brothers, his/her sisters
our	notre	notre		notre stylo, notre chaise our pen, our chair
			nos	nos stylos, nos chaises our pens, our chairs
your (pl.)	votre	votre		votre cahier, votre cousine your notebook, your cousin (f.)
			vos	vos cahiers, vos cousines your notebooks, your cousins (f.)
their	leur	leur		leur livre, leur maison their book, their house
			leurs	leurs livres, leurs maisons their books, their houses

ATTENTION!

The plural forms of the possessives printed in **bold** in the chart do not change their form to modify a masculine or a feminine noun. But these possessive forms must agree with the nouns they modify, not with the "owner" as in English.

"his house" or "her house"	= *sa maison*
"his book" or "her book"	= *son livre*

mais (but)

"his houses" or "her houses"	= *ses maisons*
"his books" or "her books"	= *ses livres*

The possessive form *ses* must be in the plural form to "agree" with the plural noun that follows and may refer to "his" or "her."

His and her depends on the gender (masculine or feminine) and number of the noun that follows.

Voici Jérôme.   Voici **son** vélo.   Voici **sa** radio.   Voici **ses** CDs.
(Here's **his** bike.) (Here's **his** radio.) (Here are **his** CDs.)

Voici Sophie.   Voici **son** vélo.   Voici **sa** radio.   Voici **ses** CDs.
(Here's **her** bike.) (Here's **her** radio.) (Here are **her** CDs.)

BRAIN TICKLERS
Set # 10

Compose the following expressions in French:

1. my brother_____

2. their house _____

3. her book _____

4. my chair _____

5. his sisters_____

6. her brothers _____

7. his sister_____

8. your (sing., fam.) pen _____

9. our school _____

10. their chairs_____

11. her sisters_____

12. his brother_____

(Answers are on page 41.)

Vive la différence!

In English we place adjectives in front of the noun, "an old cat," "a fantastic girl," but in French the placement of the adjective is generally after the noun: *une fille formidable*. In Sophie's description of her family and friends, you may have noticed that the adjectives *bon*, *petit*, and *vieux* were placed in front of the noun (*un vieux chat*), and other adjectives, such as *pénible* and *formidable*, followed the nouns. The majority of French adjectives follow the noun; however, a few adjectives almost always precede the noun. If you learn that BAGS (beauty, age, goodness, size) adjectives precede or go in front of the noun, it's easier simply to place the other adjectives after the noun.

Beauty
joli/e (pretty)
beau/belle (handsome, beautiful)

Age
jeune (young)
vieux/vieille (old)
nouveau/nouvelle (new)

Goodness
bon/ne (good)
mauvais/e (bad)
meilleur/e (better)

Size
petit/e (short, small)*
grand/e (tall/big)*
gros/grosse (fat, big)*
large (wide: for things)
long/longue (long)

* When referring to people, the adjective has the first meaning; the second meaning is used when referring to objects: *un gros homme*, a fat man; *la grosse pomme*, the big apple.

Some adjectives can be placed in either position; then their meaning changes: *un pauvre chien*, a poor, pitiful dog; *un garçon pauvre*; a poor boy, one without money.

Proverbe: Didier dit

Tout nouveau, tout beau. A new broom sweeps clean. (Literally: All new, all beautiful)

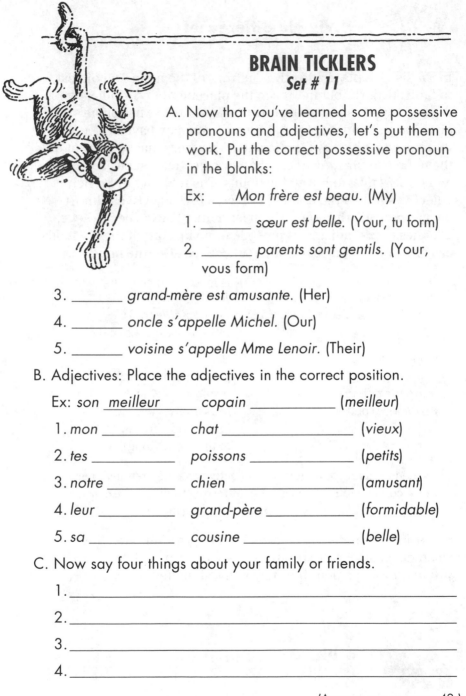

BRAIN TICKLERS
Set # 11

A. Now that you've learned some possessive pronouns and adjectives, let's put them to work. Put the correct possessive pronoun in the blanks:

Ex: ___Mon___ frère est beau. (My)

1. _____ sœur est belle. (Your, tu form)

2. _____ parents sont gentils. (Your, vous form)

3. _____ grand-mère est amusante. (Her)

4. _____ oncle s'appelle Michel. (Our)

5. _____ voisine s'appelle Mme Lenoir. (Their)

B. Adjectives: Place the adjectives in the correct position.

Ex: son _meilleur_ copain _____ (meilleur)

1. mon _____ chat _____ (vieux)

2. tes _____ poissons _____ (petits)

3. notre _____ chien _____ (amusant)

4. leur _____ grand-père _____ (formidable)

5. sa _____ cousine _____ (belle)

C. Now say four things about your family or friends.

1. _____

2. _____

3. _____

4. _____

(Answers are on page 42.)

Répète après moi!

The French r sound is distinctive, and its correct pronunciation is an important part of a good accent. Try saying "ga ga" like a baby, and place two fingers at the base of your throat. You should feel a vibration. Now say "ga ga *garage*," and try to get the r in *garage* to come from the base of your throat. Practice until you get a guttural "r."

Now say some French words with r in the spelling, like *frère*, *mère, grand-père*, or the names *Robert, Rachelle, Raoul*.

Vive la différence!

How do we say "He/She/It is_____?"
C'est* versus *Il/Elle est

In English "he" is used to describe people only. In French *il* refers to people and to masculine nouns. When you want to describe people or nouns, it is important to follow this rule:

***C'est* + noun**	***Il/Elle est* + adjective**

For example, you would say:

C'est mon frère.	He's my brother. (noun)
Il est sportif.	He's athletic. (adj.)

In English we use "he" for both sentences.

Note that if there is a noun and an adjective, use *c'est*: *C'est un garçon adorable.*

For objects, the same rule holds true:

C'est un arbre. (noun) That's a tree.

Il est vieux. (adj.) It is old.

For plural nouns, *Ce sont* and *Ils/Elles sont* are used:

Ce sont mes cousines jumelles.	*Elles sont identiques.*
They are my twin cousins.	They are identical.

Vocabulaire

Des couleurs (Colors)

Learn the following colors and remember to place them after the noun:

rose	pink	*vert/e*	green	*violet/te*	purple
rouge	red	*bleu/e*	blue	*blanc/he*	white
jaune	yellow	*noir/e*	black	*marron**	brown
beige	beige	*gris/e*	grey	*orange**	orange
*châtain**	chestnut			*brun/e*	brown
*foncé**	dark				
*clair**	light				

J'ai les cheveux châtain foncé et les yeux bleu clair.
I have dark chestnut hair and light blue eyes.

*These are invariable adjectives.

 **Proverbe: Didier dit**

La parole est d'argent, le silence est d'or.
Speech is silver, but silence is golden.

BRAIN TICKLERS
Set # 12

A. *C'est* or *il est?* Fill in *C'est* or *il est* in the following exercises:

1. _____ *français.*

2. _____ *un voisin.*

3. _____ *beau.*

4. _____ *un homme intéressant.*

B. Colors: Write in the color(s) of the following objects:

1. _____ *le ciel* (sky)

2. _____ *le soleil* (sun)

3. _____ *le dauphin* (dolphin)

4. _____ *les cerises* (cherries)

5. _____ *une moufette* (skunk)

(Answers are on page 42.)

ATTENTION!

Learning French will help you with your English. If you know that *jaune* means yellow in French, then jaundice is the illness whose symptoms include yellow skin. *Rouge* is used to mean blush or makeup that turns your cheeks red. A film noir is a movie with a dark twist; *noir* means black. Do you know the color of a verdant field? (green) What color paper is blank? (white)

Info
Les mariages français (French Weddings)

French weddings are both similar and different compared with American weddings. A wedding is an important social event in France. There are generally two wedding ceremonies. The first one is the official wedding held at the town hall. The mayor, wearing a tricolor sash, officiates in his or her office in front of a picture of the French president. The ceremony is not long, but  the wedding party signs multiple legal forms in front of their guests. The town hall may have several weddings booked for the same day, so each wedding has a color scheme. The cars all have matching ribbons to identify the wedding party and to help guests find each other. From the town hall the brightly decorated cars proceed to a church where the second ceremony is held. This ceremony is very similar to an American ceremony, except that although her father accompanies the bride down the aisle, the groom's mother also accompanies her son to the altar. After the religious ceremony the wedding party is greeted with crepe paper hearts and perhaps birdseed as they leave the church. After extensive picture taking in a picturesque setting, the reception can last all night long. The bride and groom and their guests change into evening clothes for this event. The reception hall may be decorated according to the color scheme. There are many courses of food and there is also a wedding cake. The cake may look very different. A *pièce montée* is a traditional cake that consists of a large pyramid of cream puffs held together by caramel. The reception is a joyous event that includes much laughter, singing, and dancing.

BRAIN TICKLERS
Set # 13

Read the following statements about French weddings and decide if the statement is true (vrai) or false (faux):

French weddings . . .

1. have three ceremonies. _____

2. are entirely at night. _____

3. have color schemes. _____

4. serve simple snacks after the final ceremony. _____

5. often serve a *pièce montée* for dessert. _____

(Answers are on page 42.)

A réfléchir
Le Québec

The French language came to the Americas with some of the first explorers. Jacques Cartier descended the Saint Lawrence River in 1534 and tried to persuade France to establish colonies on subsequent journeys. The harsh winters and tense relationships with the Indians (called *amérindiens* by the Canadians) discouraged colonization, and it was Samuel Champlain who succeeded in 1604 in establishing Port-Royal, then Quebec, in 1608. The fur trade, especially beaver skins used in the fabrication of the popular

Château Frontenac, Quebec City

37

hats of the time, flourished, and French explorers such as Louis Jolliet, Cavalier de la Salle, and Father Marquette pushed farther inland to explore the Great Lakes and the Mississippi River all the way to Louisiana. Wars with England and America changed the makeup of the French holdings. By 1763 France accepted England's domination of nearly all of the province of Quebec. The French Canadians maintained their language and cultural heritage throughout the rule of the English and continue to promote their unique cultural heritage on a continent where they are surrounded by English-speaking neighbors. The province of Quebec remains the largest of the ten provinces of Canada. It's three times the size of France, and Montreal is the second largest French-speaking city in the world (after Paris). Today the province of Quebec is a center of industry (especially lumber products and hydroelectric energy), tourism, culture, ethnic diversity, and innovation. French Canadians are eager to share their country with visitors and love to enjoy *la joie de vivre* of their country.

Une Carte Postale de Québec
Postcard from Quebec

Salut mon ami,

Je visite la belle province de Québec. Il fait frais et les érables (maple trees) ont déjà changé de couleur. Il y a des montagnes magnifiques couvertes de ces arbres jaunes, rouges, et même orange. Les gens d'ici parlent français 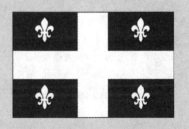 *avec un accent un peu différent, mais tout à fait charmant. Ils sont accueillants et enthousiastes quand je parle français. J'ai visité un village huron près de Québec. Là j'ai vu un village recréé du passé par les amérindiens de la région — les Hurons-Wendat. Ils font partie des Premières nations du groupe des Premières nations des régions boisées. Il y a six groupes qui habitent les six régions géographiques du Canada.*

J'adore la nourriture québécois. Pour le petit déjeuner (breakfast) les québécois disent le déjeuner. Pour le déjeuner (lunch) ils disent le dîner et pour le dîner (dinner) ils disent le souper! J'ai goûté du sirop d'érable (maple syrup) fabriqué au printemps, et de la tarte aux bluets (blueberry pie). Ce soir je vais assister à un concert de musique folklorique.

A bientôt, Sophie

For more information on the First Nations see:
https://www.aadnc-aandc.gc.ca/fra

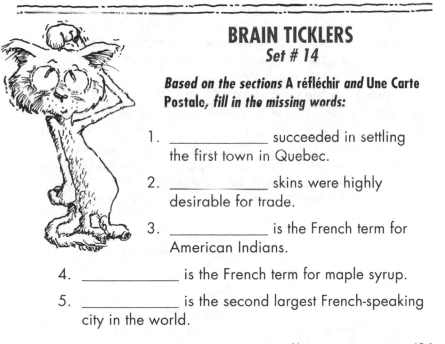

BRAIN TICKLERS
Set # 14

Based on the sections A réfléchir *and* Une Carte Postale, fill in the missing words:

1. _____ succeeded in settling the first town in Quebec.

2. _____ skins were highly desirable for trade.

3. _____ is the French term for American Indians.

4. _____ is the French term for maple syrup.

5. _____ is the second largest French-speaking city in the world.

(Answers are on page 42.)

> ### Tu sais quoi?
> ### Did you know?
>
> The term *Cajun* is derived from the displaced Acadians of Canada. In 1755, ten thousand people were separated from loved ones and sent to distant locations like the French settlement of Louisiana. They survived many hardships and learned to live in a totally new environment. Today their influence is famous for Cajun food and their motto is *"Laisser le bon temps rouler"* ("Let the good times roll").

Les Cowboys Fringants is a popular Canadian five-member néo-trad band that was formed in 1997. They are bassist Jérôme Dupras, drummer Dominique Lebeau, multi-instrumentalist Marie-Annick Lépine, guitarist Jean-François Pauzé, and vocalist Karl Tremblay. Their music is considered "Néo-trad Québécoise," which is a genre of music that combines modern Québec folk music with a rock influence. Their music carries strong messages about society and the environment in an entertaining format. In 2006, these talented musicians formed a non-profit foundation called La Fondation Cowboys Fringants. This foundation promotes the protection of fragile eco-systems, supports scientific research, and educates the public at large about its responsibility to the Earth. The website for the foundation is: *http://fondation.cowboysfringants.com/la-fondation/*

You can find many videos as well as song lyrics on YouTube or at *http://www.cowboysfringants.com/*

Another interesting néo-trad group is Mes Aïeux: *https://fr-ca.facebook.com/mesaieux*

The Québecois style of French is quite different from traditional French. Here is a list of some expressions you may find in their songs

la bouffe	food
Mon chum	my friend
Ma blonde	my girlfriend
Chu	I am (Je suis)
frette	cold (froid)
moé	me (moi)
pis	then/and
tsé	you know (tu sais)

To look up more French Canadian expressions, try the search box at: *http://offqc.com/*

 **Amis/Faux Amis**

In this chapter you recognized many *amis*, or cognates, French words that are identical or similar in spelling and meaning to the English words. **La niece, le cousin, l'oncle, la table,** and **bleu** are good examples.

Did you notice these **faux amis** or "false friends"?

Grand/grande in French means "tall" in describing people.
Large means "wide" in French.
Jolie means "pretty," not jolly.
Marron means "brown," not maroon or dark red.
Parents means "parents," but also refers to relatives in general.

BRAIN TICKLERS—THE ANSWERS

Set # 8, page 25
1. *le*
2. *le*
3. *la*
4. *la*
5. *l'*
6. *l'*
7. *le*
8. *la*
9. *la*
10. *le*

Set # 9, page 27
1. *une tablette*
2. *les livres*
3. *l'école*

4. *des cahiers*
5. *un portable*
6. *une salle de classe*
7. *des tablettes*
8. *un stylo*
9. *les écoles*
10. *le portable*

Set # 10, page 30
1. *mon frère*
2. *leur maison*
3. *son livre*
4. *ma chaise*
5. *ses sœurs*
6. *ses frères*
7. *sa sœur*

8. *ton stylo*
9. *notre école*
10. *leurs chaises*
11. *ses sœurs*
12. *son frère*

Set # 11, page 32
A.
1. *ta*
2. *vos*
3. *sa*
4. *notre*
5. *leur*

B.
1. *mon vieux chat*
2. *tes petits poissons*
3. *notre chien amusant*
4. *leur grand-père formidable*
5. *sa belle cousine*

C.
Answers will vary.

Set # 12, page 35
A.
1. *Il est français.*
2. *C'est un voisin.*
3. *Il est beau.*
4. *C'est un homme intéressant.*

B.
1. *bleu*
2. *jaune*
3. *gris*
4. *rouges*
5. *blanche et noire*

Set # 13, page 37
1. *faux*
2. *faux*
3. *vrai*
4. *faux*
5. *vrai*

Set # 14, page 39
1. Samuel Champlain
2. Beaver
3. *Amérindiens*
4. *Sirop d'étable*
5. *Montréal*

J'habite ici: Mon appartement et ma ville

THIS IS WHERE I LIVE: MY APARTMENT AND MY TOWN

Salut! C'est Sophie. Ça va? Comme tu sais, j'habite à Paris dans un appartement classique. Il y a des plafonds hauts et des planchers en bois ciré. Nous avons six pièces avec WC et une salle de bain. Il y a trois chambres à coucher, un salon, une salle à manger, et une cuisine. Nous n'avons pas de jardin, mais il y a un cour a l'arrière. Dans ma chambre, j'ai une télé, une armoire, un bureau, et une chaise. Mon chien Max aime dormir sur mon lit. Les murs sont jaunes et j'ai quelques affiches d'animaux. Je fais mes devoirs et lis dans ma chambre. J'aime notre appartement au troisième étage, mais j'adore la maison de mes grands-parents en banlieue. Le dimanche nous allons chez eux. Ils ont une petite maison de deux étages avec un joli jardin. Au rez-de-chaussée il y a un salon avec une vieille cheminée. Dans notre quartier il y a une épicerie en face de notre immeuble, à gauche de l'épicerie il y a une boulangerie-pâtisserie, et au coin il y a une quincaillerie. Un peu plus loin il y a un supermarché et une librairie. La station de métro se trouve à cinq minutes de chez nous. C'est un quartier très pratique.

Vocabulaire

Le domicile	Home
le domicile	residence; home
l'appartement	apartment
l'immeuble	apartment building
la maison	house
en ville	in town
en banlieue	in the suburbs
le jardin	garden
le cours	courtyard
le rez-de-chaussée	ground floor

le premier étage	first floor up (English usage second floor)
le troisième étage	third floor up (English usage fourth floor)
les pièces	rooms
la cuisine	kitchen
la chambre à coucher	bedroom
le salon	living room
la salle à manger	dining room
la cheminée	fireplace
la salle de bains	bathroom
le WC (water closet)	toilet; half bath
le plafond	ceiling
le plancher	floor
le mur	wall
chez moi	my house/at my home
chez nous	our house/at our home
Les meubles	**Furniture**
l'armoire	armoire (free-standing closet)
le bureau	desk
la chaise	chair
le fauteuil	armchair
le lit	bed
les rideaux	curtains
le sofa, le canapé	sofa
la table	table
la télévision, la télé	television, TV
le téléviseur	television set

Le quartier	Neighborhood
le métro	subway
l'hôtel	hotel
la ville	town, city
la banque	bank
le bureau	office
le centre commercial	shopping center, mall, office park
l'hôpital	hospital
la pharmacie	pharmacy
la poste	post office
la quincaillerie	hardware store
le supermarché	supermarket
le hypermarché	superstore
la boucherie	butcher shop
la boulangerie	bakery
la pâtisserie	pastry shop
la charcuterie	deli/prepared meat
l'épicerie	grocery

 ## Vive la différence!

In French, the first or ground floor is called the *rez-de-chaussée*. In the vocabulary list, *le premier étage* is defined as "the first floor up," or what would designate the second floor in English usage. *Le troisième étage* designates the third floor above the *rez-de-chaussée*, or what would be the fourth floor to an English speaker, and so on.

Other differences to notice: *la salle de bains* means a true bathroom, where one may take a bath or shower. If you are asking to find the restroom, ask for *la toilette* or for the *WC*, not the *salle de bains*.

Grammaire
Conjugating Verbs in the Present Tense

In French as in English, we need to use **verbs**, the words that express action or state of being, to make statements, to pose questions, or to make commands. In Chapter 1, you learned the forms for the irregular verbs *être* and *avoir*. In this section we introduce the present tense forms of three main categories, or conjugations, of regular French verbs.

First Conjugation: Infinitive ends in **-er**

habiter	to live	*travailler*	to work
jouer	to play	*écouter*	to listen to
chanter	to sing	*aimer*	to like, to love
parler	to speak	*danser*	to dance
étudier	to study	*penser*	to think
regarder	to look at		

Second Conjugation: Infinitive ends in **-ir**

finir	to finish	*choisir*	to choose
réussir	to succeed	*grossir*	to gain weight

Third Conjugation: Infinitive ends in **-re**

vendre	to sell	*entendre*	to hear
perdre	to lose	*attendre*	to wait
répondre	to answer		

The present indicative tense is used to express what is happening now or what is universally true. The present indicative of *parler*, for example, is translated in English as **I speak, I do speak** (emphatic), or **I am speaking** (progressive), **You speak . . . do speak . . . are speaking, etc.** The verb is conjugated by dropping the **-er, -ir,** or **-re** infinitive ending to create the stem, then adding the appropriate endings, shown here in bold:

	First conjugation	Second conjugation	Third conjugation
Singular			
Je	parl-**e**	fin-**is**	vend-**s**
Tu	parl-**es**	fin-**is**	vend-**s**
Elle/il	parl-**e**	fin-**it**	vend*
Plural			
Nous	parl-**ons**	fin-**issons**	vend-**ons**
Vous	parl-**ez**	fin-**issez**	vend-**ez**
Elles/ils	parl-**ent**	fin-**issent**	vend-**ent**

*Third conjugation verbs whose stem ends in a letter other than -d usually add -t here:

interrompre   il interrompt

BRAIN TICKLERS
Set # 15

With the verb chart as a guide, write the correct French form for the following expressions. The infinitive forms were listed earlier.

1. You (pl.) are speaking
2. They work (f.)
3. I hear
4. We live
5. He sells
6. I lose
7. She likes
8. You (sing.) work
9. They are gaining weight
10. You (pl.) are finishing

(Answers are on page 69.)

49

Grammaire
The Imperative Mood

The present indicative voice just introduced is also used for the imperative, to give commands or make requests. The imperative forms are those of the second person (or "you" forms , both singular and plural) and first person plural (or "we" forms), generally translated as "let us . . ." or "let's." In the first conjugation, the *tu* form drops the **-s.** The subject pronouns are in parentheses because the subject pronoun is not expressed in the imperative mood. In English we refer to this as the "you understood."

(Tu)	parl**e**	fin**is**	vend**s**
(Vous)	parl**ez**	fin**issez**	vend**ez**
(Nous)	parl**ons**	fin**issons**	vend**ons**

Here are some examples:

Parle! (sing.)	(you) Speak!
Travaillons	Let's work . . .
Finis ton travail, finissez votre travail	Finish your work
Réussissons	Let's succeed
Attendez (you, pl.)	Wait! Please wait . . .

Grammaire
Using Inversion to Ask a Question

One simple way to pose a question in French is to invert the indicative word order. Here are some familiar examples:

Parlez-vous?	*Chantez-vous?*

Grammaire
Negative Expressions

The negative in French is generally formed in two parts. We use **ne** (verb) **pas** to express the simple negative of most verb forms:

Je ne travaille pas	I do not work, I am not working
Il ne parle pas	He does not speak, he is not speaking
Nous n'attendons pas	We are not waiting

Note: *ne* **becomes** *n'* **when it precedes a verb that begins with a vowel or silent** *-h*:

Elle n'habite pas ici.	She does not live here.
N'attendez pas!	Don't (you) wait! (Imperative)

BRAIN TICKLERS
Set # 16

Write the following expressions in French:

1. I am not watching TV.
2. They (*elles*) do not live here.
3. Let's not wait!
4. You (*Tu*) are answering
5. We do not work here.
6. I am studying.
7. (You, pl.) Finish!
8. We are selling our apartment.
9. She works at the bookstore.
10. They (*Ils*) are studying.

(Answers are on page 70.)

Vive la différence!

Writing the date

dimanche le premier janvier, 2017	Sunday, January 1, 2017
samedi le quatorze juillet, 2018	Saturday, July 14, 2018
lundi le huit octobre, 2018	Monday, October 8, 2018

Note that names of the days and the months are not capitalized in French.

In French the day (*le jour*) is given first, followed by the month (*le mois*), and finally by the year (*l'année* or *l'an*). The word for century is *la siècle*.

When you write the abbreviated numerical date in French, you must also put the day first:

15/1/17   4/7/18   22/11/19

Finally, if you look at a French calendar, you will see that the French week (*la semaine*) starts with Monday (*lundi*) and ends with *dimanche* (Sunday).

Vocabulaire

The French calendar is easy to learn if you remember names of the planets or mythology. Like the planets, most of the days of the week are named for ancient Roman gods:

lundi	Monday: moon day (*lune*)
mardi	Tuesday: Mars's day
mercredi	Wednesday: Mercury's day
jeudi	Thursday: Jupiter's day
vendredi	Friday: Venus's day
samedi	Saturday: Sabbath day
dimanche	Sunday: the Lord's day

The months of the year also are named for Romans and their gods:

janvier	January: Janus
février	February: month of purification
mars	March: Mars
avril	April: Aphrodite
mai	May: Maia, daughter of Atlas
juin	June: Junon, Italian goddess
juillet	July: Julius Caesar (a Roman emperor)

août	August: Augustus (a Roman emperor)
septembre	September: septième mois (7th month of the Roman calendar)
octobre	October: huitième mois (8th month of the Roman calendar)
novembre	November: neuvième mois (9th month of the Roman calendar)
décembre	December: dixième mois (10th month of the Roman calendar)

ATTENTION!

Septième, huitième, neuvième, and *dixième* are ordinal numbers used to designate seventh, eighth, ninth, and tenth. They are formed by adding the suffix *–ième* to most cardinal numbers, for example: *deux* (two), *deuxième; trois* (three), *troisième.*

If the number ends in e, drop the silent e: *quatre, quatrième; onze, onzième.*

Add u to q: *cinq, cinquième,* and change f to v: *neuf, neuvième.*

Ordinal numbers are not used for the date except for the first of the month: *le premier avril.* The other days of the month use cardinal numbers: *le deux juin, le huit mai, le trente et un octobre.*

The cardinal numbers in French were introduced in Chapter 1. Here is a chart to show you how ordinal numbers are formed.

Cardinal Numbers		Ordinal Numbers	
one	*un, une*	first	*premier*
two	*deux*	second	*second/deuxième**
three	*trois*	third	*troisième*
four	*quatre*	fourth	*quatrième*
five	*cinq*	fifth	*cinquième*
six	*six*	sixth	*sixième*

seven	sept	seventh	septième
eight	huit	eighth	huitième
nine	neuf	ninth	neuvième
ten	dix	tenth	dixième
twenty	vingt	twentieth	vingtième
twenty-one	vingt et un	twenty-first	vingt et unième
twenty-two	vingt-deux	twenty-second	vingt-deuxième
thirty	trente	thirtieth	trentième
thirty-one	trente et un	thirty-first	trente et unième

*Second is used if there are only two parts

Proverbe: Didier dit

C'est le premier pas qui coûte. It's the first step that counts. (Literally: It is the first step that costs.)

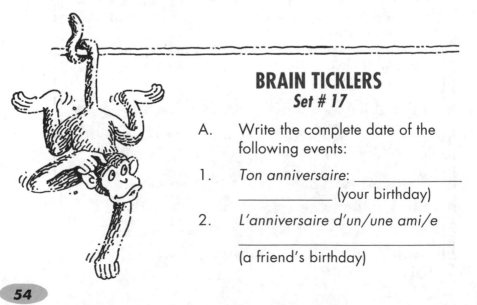

BRAIN TICKLERS
Set # 17

A. Write the complete date of the following events:

1. *Ton anniversaire:* _____ _____ (your birthday)

2. *L'anniversaire d'un/une ami/e*

_____

(a friend's birthday)

3. *Le premier jour de l'école* _____
   (first day of school)

4. *Le jour de l'an:* _____
   (New Year's Day)

5. *Le jour de saint Valentin:* _____
   (Valentine's Day)

B. Give the ordinal numbers for the following:

1. First _____

2. Sixth _____

3. Fifteenth _____

4. Twentieth _____

5. Ninth _____

C. Fill in the missing months for the four seasons. Practice saying the seasons and months out loud until you can do it without looking:

le printemps	*l'été*	*l'automne*	*l'hiver*
spring	summer	fall	winter
m _____	j _____	s _____	d _____
a _____	j _____	o _____	j _____
m _____	a _____	n _____	f _____

(Answers are on page 70.)

Quelle heure est-il?
Telling Time in French

To say it is one o'clock, a French person would say, **Il est une heure**. To indicate morning, he or she would add, **du matin**. For the afternoon, he could say, **Il est une heure de l'après-midi**, or use the 24-hour method (military time): *Il est **treize** heures.* (12 + 1 = **13**) For eight o'clock, she could say, *Il est huit heures* **du soir** (evening) or *Il est vingt heures.* (20h).

When referring to official time, schedules, and so on, the military or 24-hour clock is used: *Le film commence à 21h* (9 PM) *et finit à 23h30 (vingt-trois heures trente, 11:30 PM).*

Encore c'est mieux
Other Useful Expressions

tôt	early
tard	late

être en avance	to be early
être à l'heure	to be on time
être en retard	to be late

Proverbe: Didier dit

Mieux vaut tard que jamais. Better late than never.

To indicate minutes before or after the hour in conversational French, study the following chart:

1:00 *Il est **une** heure.*

2:05 *Il est **deux** heure**s** cinq.*

3:20 *Il est **trois** heures **vingt**.*

4:15 *Il est **quatre** heure**s** **et quart**. (Il est quatre heures quinze.)*

6:30 *Il est six heures **et demie**. (Il est six heures trente.)*

When the time is after the half hour, use ***moins*** to express how many minutes remain until the next hour:

7:35 *Il est **huit** heures **moins vingt-cinq**. (Il est sept heures trente-cinq.)*

8:45 *Il est **neuf** heures **moins le quart**. (Il est huit heures quarante-cinq.)*

9:50 *Il est **dix** heures **moins dix**. (Il est neuf heures cinquante.)*

12:00 ***Il est midi**. (noon)*
   ***Il est minuit**. (midnight) or **24h00** (Il est **vingt-quatre** heures.)*

Attention: 12:30 *Il est midi et **demi*** or *Il est minuit et **demi**.*

Note that the expression *douze heures* is never used in conversational time.

***A quelle heure** est le film?* (What time is the movie?) *Le film est à vingt heures dix.* (8:10 PM)
Use *à quelle heure?* to ask when an event takes place.

BRAIN TICKLERS
Set # 18

A. At what time do you do the following?
(Use conversational French expressions.)
A quelle heure est-ce que tu . . .

1. *prends le petit déjeuner*
(eat breakfast)

2. *déjeunes* (eat lunch)

3. *dînes* (eat dinner)

4. *fais tes devoirs* (do your homework)

5. *te couches* (go to bed)

B. Spell out the following times, then convert to AM/PM times:

Ex. Strasbourg? 14.15 … à quatorze heures quinze/2:15 PM

À quelle heure est le train pour:

1. *Toulouse?* 05.00: à_____ /
2. *Nice?* 07.20: à_____ /_____
3. *Bordeaux?* 13.40: à_____ /_____
4. *Reims?* 19.30: à _____ /_____
5. *Pau?* 20.55: à _____ /_____

(Answers are on page 70.)

Grammaire
Les prépositions

To describe where things are located in your room, house, or
town, you will need to learn some prepositions:

dans	in, within
devant	in front of
derrière	behind
sous	under
sur	on
entre	between

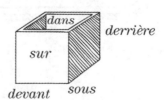

Imagine putting the word *devant*, "in front," of the longer word *derrière* "behind":

Encore c'est mieux
Prepositions in Phrases

Many prepositions require the word *de* and its contractions. When giving directions, you may say *tournez à gauche* (turn left), or *c'est à côté* (it's next door). But you need to know the gender and number of the following word if you are talking about a location's relation to another.

à gauche de, de la, du, de l', des	to the left of
à droite de	to the right of
en face de	across from
à côté de	next to
loin de	far from
près de	near to
au coin de	on the corner of

ATTENTION!

The words *de* + definite articles follow the chart you learned earlier with a couple of contractions:

de + le = du
de + les = des
de la and *de l'* remain two words. They all mean "from the" or "of the."

Le restaurant se trouve **au coin de la rue** Lafayette. J'habite **en face de l'école, à droite du lycée**, et **loin des magasins**.

BRAIN TICKLERS
Set # 19

A. Use prepositions to describe this bedroom.

1. *Mon lit est _____ une affiche.* (under)

2. *La fenêtre est _____ mon bureau.* (behind)

3. *Mon bureau est _____ le mur.* (in front of)

4. *Il y a une lampe _____ la table.* (on)

5. *Mes livres sont _____ mon sac à dos.* (backpack) (in)

B. Can you think of five places in town and their distances from your house?

Ex: *La banque est près de chez moi.*

1. _____ est _____ de chez moi.

2. _____ est _____ de chez moi.

3. _____ est _____ de chez moi.

4. _____ est _____ de chez moi.

5. _____ est _____ de chez moi.

C. Write in the correct form of *de* plus the article:

1. *Le centre commercial se trouve loin _____ hôpital.*

2. *L'école se trouve en face _____ parc.*

3. *La poste se trouve à côté _____ banque.*

4. *La station de métro se trouve près _____ magasins.*

(Answers are on page 70.)

Répète après moi!

You may have noticed that there are several variations for the -ay sound in French. For example, *Parlez-vous français*? The following words contain the -ay sound. Pronounce them with your mouth slightly closed and your tongue down behind your teeth. Keep the sound fairly tight. Don't stretch it out or distort it.

> ai: j'ai
> é: café
> et: croquet
> er: donner
> ez: dansez

Try: ***Renée voudrait danser au café. S'il vous plaît.***

Grammaire

Le passé composé is used to talk about a completed action in the past: *J'ai mangé*: I ate, I have eaten, I did eat. It is a **past tense** that is composed of two parts: a helping verb plus a past participle.

Most verbs use the present tense of *avoir*, but a few use *être*. We'll look at those later in the chapter.

To form the past participle of a regular verb, study the following:

-er verbs, é	parler	parlé
-ir verbs, i	finir	fini
-re verbs, u	vendre	vendu

J'ai parlé français.	I spoke French.
Tu as dansé au bal.	You danced at the dance.
Il a regardé le canard.	He watched the duck.
Elle a chanté au concert.	She sang in the concert.
Nous avons attendu cinq minutes.	We waited five minutes.
Vous avez perdu le match.	You lost the game.
Ils ont fini tard.	They finished late.
Elles ont grossi en été.	They gained weight in the summer.

To express the sentence in the negative, make the helping verb negative:

*Tu **n'as pas vendu** ton vélo.*   You didn't sell your bike.

To ask a question with inversion, invert the helping verb:

As-tu rangé *ta chambre?*   Did you straighten your room?

Vocabulaire

Here are a few helpful expressions that indicate the past:

hier	yesterday
en 2000	in 2000
hier soir	last night
il y a dix minutes	ten minutes ago
hier matin	yesterday morning
il y a cinq ans	five years ago
la semaine dernière	last week
il y a trois siècles	three centuries ago
le week-end dernier	last weekend
en mai	in May
vendredi dernier	last Friday
l'année dernière	last year

Grammaire

Sixteen verbs in the passé composé are conjugated with *être*. Most of them have to do with motion:

Je suis allé au zoo. I went to the zoo.

Tu es resté à la maison. You stayed home.

One way of memorizing the verbs is this mnemonic device: "Dr. and Mrs. Vandertramp."

devenir   to become:
Je suis devenu prof. I became a teacher.

revenir   to come back:
Tu es revenu en taxi. You came back in a taxi.

monter   to go up:
Il est monté sur le toit. He went up on the roof.

rester   to stay:
Elle est restée* au lit. She stayed in bed.

sortir   to go out:
Nous sommes sortis* ensemble. We went out together.

venir   to come:
Vous êtes venus* chez moi. You came to my house.

aller   to go:
Ils sont allés* au stade. They went to the stadium.

naître   to be born:
Elles sont nées* en Chine. They were born in China.

descendre   to go down:
Je suis descendue* dans la cave. I went down to the cellar.

entrer   to enter:
Tu es entrée* dans le café. You entered the café.

rentrer   to go home:
Il est rentré lentement. He went home slowly.

tomber   to fall:
Elle est tombée* dans le lac. She fell in the lake.

retourner   to return:
Nous sommes retournés* tard. We returned late.

arriver   to arrive:
Vous êtes arrivés* à l'heure. You arrived on time.

mourir   to die:
Les arbres sont morts.* The trees died.

partir   to leave:
Les filles sont parties* à minuit. The girls left at midnight.

*When verbs are conjugated with *être*, the past participles are treated like adjectives. This means they must agree in gender and number with the subject of the verb. Notice the asterisks on the participles. You can see which subjects are feminine singular or plural and which are masculine singular or plural.

ATTENTION!

Passer can be used in two ways. When it is used to mean "to pass by" (as an intransitive verb), the passé composé is formed with *être*:

> *Je suis passé par le parc.*
> I passed by the park.

When it takes an object (as a transitive verb) and means to spend time, to take an examination, and so on, then the passé composé is formed with *avoir*.

> *J'ai passé l'été chez ma grand-mère. Nous avons passé les soirs sous les étoiles.*
> I spent the summer at my grandmother's house. We spent the evenings under the stars.

BRAIN TICKLERS
Set # 20

A. Give the correct forms of the passé composé for these *avoir* verbs:

Ex: *Elle **a dansé** avec Pierre.* (danced)

1. *Ce matin tu _____ le croissant.* (chose)

2. *Hier, nous _____ notre argent* (our money). (lost)

3. *Après les classes, ils _____ _____ le métro.* (waited for)

4. *La semaine dernière vous* _____
   "La Marseillaise." (sang)

5. *Je* _____ *l'escargot.* (didn't eat)

B. Now write these verbs in the passé composé using the helping verb *être*:

> Ex: *Ils **sont tombés** de leurs chaises.* (tomber)
> (They fell off their chairs.)

1. *Tu* (f.) _____
   ce matin. (sortir)

2. *Ton père* _____
   hier soir. (rentrer)

3. *Il y a dix ans ta mère* _____
   avocate. (devenir)

4. *Tes grands-parents* _____
   du cinéma après le film. (retourner)

5. *Ton chien* _____
   sur le divan. (monter)

6. *Samedi dernier tes sœurs* _____
   au centre commercial. (aller)

C. Now write five sentences in the passé composé about what you did last weekend.

Make sure to use words from the list to say when you did the activities.

1. _____
2. _____
3. _____
4. _____
5. _____

(Answers are on page 70.)

Répète après moi!

As you practice writing the Brain Ticklers, say the sentences out loud and practice your pronunciation. Pay attention to liaison. There are many rules that govern the liaison, which is the sliding of one word into another, but the most important one at this time is between the subject pronoun and the verb:

Vous allez	(vou zah lay)
Ils ont	(eel zon)
Il est allé	(eel eh ta lay)

A réfléchir
La Martinique

Did you know that the islands of Martinique and Guadaloupe in the Carribean have been overseas departments of France since 1946? Christopher Columbus's arrival in 1502 started a chain of wars for the domination of the islands. The islands were fought over by the English, the Dutch, and the French. France gained ownership and is still (by a referendum voted on by the people) the governing country. Martinique is represented by four deputies and two senators in France. Slaves were imported from Africa to work on Martinique, and sugarcane cultivation was started in 1638. In 1848 the slaves revolted and became free. Their lives were still hard as independent workers, and many worked and died in the sugarcane fields. Today  the people of Martinique are proud of their culture and customs. They enjoy the abundant seafood, fruits such as *les mangues* (mangoes), *les ananas* (pineapples), and *les noix de coco* (cocoa nuts), and vegetables such as *les patates douces* (sweet potatoes). They speak Créole and French, and their music is a joyful melodic combination called Zouk. For Carnival, or Mardi Gras, the celebration lasts five days, and participants often dress in red with devil masks for Mardi Gras ("Fat Tuesday"). Martinique is only 70 km (44 mi) long and 30 km (18.6 mi) wide, but there is a rich variety to be explored. The northern part of the island is home to Mont Pelée, a volcano that erupted in 1902. Nearby you can walk on dazzling black beaches. The central section of Martinique is made up of plains, and there are banana, pineapple, and sugarcane plantations. Most of the population lives in the southern part of the island where the white beaches and stunning coves are favorite destinations for locals and tourists alike. There are many ocean activities to try, like kite surfing and scuba diving. Inland there are lush trails that pass by natural wonders such as waterfalls and breathtaking views. The flowers, butterflies, and hummingbirds seem to echo the atmosphere of *Vivre comme il vous plait* (Live the way you wish) so popular on the island of Martinique.

Une Carte Postale de Martinique

Salut mon ami,

Je suis arrivée en Martinique il y a une semaine et j'ai beaucoup de choses à écrire. D'abord mon oncle Raoul m'a rencontrée à l'aéroport. Oncle Raoul est le frère de mon père, et il habite actuellement à Fort de France, la capitale de la Martinique. Nous sommes retournés chez lui et j'ai dormi pendant tout l'après midi. Le jour suivant (the following day) nous avons visité les monuments principaux de Fort de France. J'ai aimé le marché en plein air. J'ai acheté des souvenirs et j'ai pris beaucoup de photos. Nous avons mangé des langoustines (prawns) et après j'ai choisi une glace au noix de coco. Dimanche Oncle Raoul a invité des amis à dîner chez lui. Les Martiniquais sont très gentils. Ils ont joué de la musique Zouk et m'ont enseigné à danser. Lundi dernier nous sommes allés au nord pour visiter la Montagne Pelée. C'est un volcan qui a explosé en 1902 et a détruit la ville de St Pierre. Une personne a survécu (survived) parce qu'il a été en prison, le bâtiment le plus solide de la ville! Je suis très fatiguée ce soir parce que nous avons fait de la voile aujourd'hui.

A bientôt, Sophie

BRAIN TICKLERS
Set # 21

Reread A Réfléchir **and the** Carte Postale de Martinique, **and answer these questions in French:**

1. *Qui a découvert la Martinique?*
2. *Quelle est la longueur de l'île?*
3. *Quelles sont des fruits produits en Martinique?*
4. *Comment s'appelle la musique de la Martinique?*
5. *Quand est-ce que le volcan Mont Pelée a explosé?*

(Answers are on page 70.)

Tu sais quoi?

Napoleon Bonaparte's first wife, Joséphine (née Marie Josèphe Rose Tascher de la Pagerie), was born in Martinique. When she met Napoleon she was a divorcée with two children. He was very much in love with her and crowned her empress when he crowned himself emperor in 1804 in Notre Dame de Paris. Unfortunately, when she was unable to have his children he divorced her. To have heirs for his empire he married his second wife, Marie Louise of Austria. Napoleon and Joséphine remained friends. Joséphine's family plantation was destroyed by a hurricane, yet tourists may still visit the remains to see artifacts from her life.

Un poète antillais: Daniel Thaly

In the early 1900s, black poets from around the world started writing of their heritage. The movement is called *négritude*. Daniel Thaly was born in Dominica in 1878. He went to school in

Martinique and studied medicine in Toulouse, France. His great love was literature, and he wrote poems, books, and anthologies from 1899 until 1948. He wrote of visions of Africa and his love of the islands. The following is an excerpt from *L'île lointaine* (The Faraway Island).

L'île lointaine

Je suis né dans une île amoureuse du vent
Où l'air à des odeurs de sucre et de vanille
Et que berce au soleil du tropique mouvant
Les flots tièdes et bleus de la mer des Antilles

Sous les brises au chant des arbres familiers
J'ai vu les horizons où planent les frégates
Et respirer l'encens sauvage des halliers
Dans ses forêts pleines de fleurs et d'aromates

—*Daniel Thaly*

Vocabulaire

amoureuse	in love
du vent	with the wind
vanille	vanilla
berce	rocks (verb: *bercer*)
soleil	sun
flots	waves
brises	breezes
j'ai vu	I saw

planent, planer	to glide
respirer	to breathe
sauvage	wild
halliers	shrubbery

Amis/Faux Amis

In this chapter you probably recognized many additional *amis*, words in French that are similar or identical in spelling and meaning to their English counterparts: *l'appartement, la table, l'hôpital, danser, arriver,* are just a few examples; note also that the names of the months in French are close cognates.

Did you notice these *faux amis*, or "false friends"?

Attendre means "to wait for," not "to attend."

Football refers to the game of soccer in France and in most of the world outside the United States.

Librairie means "bookstore" in French; a library is une bibliothèque.

Location means a "rental" in French; the verb louer means "to rent."

Passer means "to pass by" in English, but to *passer un examen* means "to take" an exam; "to pass" in French is *réussir à un examen.*

Sauvage means "wild" in French; in French we use brutal or brute to mean "savage."

Visiter means "to visit" in French, but it is used only for places, such as a museum, and not for visits to friends or family.

BRAIN TICKLERS — THE ANSWERS

Set # 15, page 49

1. *vous parlez*
2. *elles travaillent*
3. *j'entends*
4. *nous habitons*
5. *il vend*
6. *je perds*
7. *elle aime*
8. *tu travailles*
9. *ils grossissent*
10. *vous finissez*

Set # 16, page 51

1. *Je ne regarde pas la télé.*
2. *Elles n'habitent pas ici.*
3. *N'attendons pas!*
4. *Tu réponds.*
5. *Nous ne travaillons pas ici.*
6. *J'étudie.*
7. *Finissez!*
8. *Nous vendons notre appartement.*
9. *Elle travaille à la librairie.*
10. *Ils étudient.*

Set # 17, page 54

A.

1–3. Answers will vary.
4. *le premier janvier*
5. *le quatorze février*

B.

1. *premier*
2. *sixième*
3. *quinzième*
4. *vingtième*
5. *neuvième*

C.

mars	juin	septembre	décembre
avril	juillet	octobre	janvier
mai	août	novembre	février

Set # 18, page 57

A.

Answers will vary.

B.

1. *cinq heures/*5 AM
2. *sept heures vingt/*7:20 AM
3. *treize heures quarante/* 1:40 PM
4. *neuf heures trente/*7:30 PM
5. *vingt heures cinquante-cinq/*8:55 PM

Set # 19, page 59

A.

1. *sous*
2. *derrière*
3. *devant*
4. *sur*
5. *dans*

B.

Answers will vary.

C.

1. *de l'(hôpital)*
2. *du (parc)*
3. *de la (banque)*
4. *des (magasins)*

Set # 20, page 63

A.

1. *as choisi*
2. *avons perdu*
3. *ont attendu*
4. *avez chanté*
5. *n'ai pas mangé*

B.

1. *es sortie*
2. *est resté*
3. *est devenue*
4. *sont retournés*
5. *est monté*
6. *sont allées*

C.

Answers will vary.

Set # 21, page 67

1. Christopher Columbus
2. 70 km (44 mi)
3. *les ananas, les noix de coco, et les mangues*
4. Zouk
5. 1902

Ce que j'aime faire:
Nos activités

WHAT I LIKE TO DO: ACTIVITIES

Salut! C'est Sophie. Comment ça va? Qu'est-ce que tu aimes faire quand tu as du temps libre? Où est-ce que tu aimes aller pendant les vacances? Moi, je suis assez sportive; alors, après l'école j'essaie de faire une activité physique. J'aime sortir en plein air pour changer des idées et m'amuser. En général je fais du vélo ou du roller dans mon quartier. Pendant l'été ma famille et moi allons à la plage pour le mois d'août. Nous allons chez ma grand-mère sur l'Ile de Ré sur la côte Atlantique. C'est super joli. Là j'aime me bronzer et nager avec mes cousins quand il fait chaud. S'il fait du vent je fais de la voile avec mon père, mais mon frère Jean-Luc préfère faire de la planche à voile. C'est un sport fascinant. Je voudrais apprendre à le faire l'année prochaine. Mes parents font du vélo et de la marche. Pendant l'année scolaire mon frère joue au foot et je fais des leçons de flûte. J'aime aussi lire et écrire du courrier électronique à mes copines. Ni mon frère ni moi ne travaillons. Les études sont trop importantes et nos parents préfèrent que nous étudiions le soir. A bientôt, Sophie

Vocabulaire

Les sports	Sports
le basket	basketball
la gymnastique	gymnastics
la marche	walking
l'escrime	fencing
le foot	soccer
le cyclisme	biking/cycling
le golf	golf
la natation	swimming
le patinage	skating
le ski	skiing
le jogging	jogging
la pèche	fishing

le tennis	tennis
la pelote	jai alai
la planche à voile	windsurfing
le volley	volleyball
la voile	sailing
l'athlétisme	track and field
les sports d'hiver	winter sports

Miscellanées / Miscellaneous

une équipe	a team
un coureur	a runner
un joueur/une joueuse	a player (m/f)
un match	a game
un match nul	a tie game
un tournoi	a tournament
un championnat	a championship
le résultat	result, outcome
un maillot	a jersey
une balle	a ball (for games such as tennis, ping-pong, children's games)
un ballon	a ball (inflated, such as for soccer, basketball, football, etc.)
un gymnase	a gym, gymnasium
un stade	a stadium
marquer un but	to score a goal

gagner	to win	le gagnant	winner
perdre	to lose	le perdant	loser

Les loisirs / Pastimes and Activities

faire de l'escalade	to climb
nager	to swim

courir	to run		
écrire	to write		
lire	to read	*la lecture*	reading
dessiner	to draw	*le dessin*	drawing
peindre	to paint	*la peinture*	painting
patiner	to skate	*le patinage*	skating
faire de la photographie *or de la photo*	to do photography		
jouer du piano, de la *guitare*	to play piano, guitar		
jouer aux jeux-vidéo	to play video games		
lire un roman, *une histoire*	to read a novel, a history, or story		
voir un film/aller *au cinéma*	to see a movie/ go to the movies		

Info

The French are avid fans of movies—*le cinéma*—and American movies are especially popular. Listings for foreign films in France include (vo), *version originale*, or (vf), *version française*, indicating whether a film is in the original language, with French subtitles, or dubbed in French.

un dessin animé	animated cartoon
une bande dessinée	comic strip
un film/roman d'amour	romance movie/novel
un film/roman d'aventure	adventure movie/novel
un film/roman d'horreur	horror movie/novel
un film/roman de science fiction	science fiction movie/novel
un western	cowboy movie, a "western"

Pour décrire	**Description**
fascinant/e	fascinating
génial/e	awesome

intéressant/e	interesting
passionnant/e	enthralling
beau (bel, belle)	beautiful
ravissant/e	charming, very pleasing
ennuyeux, ennuyeuse	boring
embêtant/e	annoying

RAPPEL!

Remember that adjectives must agree with the nouns they modify. So, we would say, **un film intéressant**, **ravissant**, but **une histoire intéressante**, **fascinante**.

ATTENTION!

Jouer au *football américain* is the act of playing the game:

Je joue au football américain cet après-midi.
I am playing football this afternoon.

Faire du *football américain* expresses what you do in general, without reference to a specific time:

Jean-Luc fait du football américain avec ses amis.
Jean-Luc plays American football with his friends.

Remember to use **au** with *jouer* and **du** with *faire*:

*Je joue **au** tennis.*   *Je fais **du** tennis.*

Lacrosse is an exception: *Je joue à lacrosse* or *Je fais de lacrosse.*

Why did we refer to *football américain*? Remember that soccer is probably the most popular sport around the world, and in French, **soccer** is **le football**, or **le foot**. Sophie told us earlier that her brother Jean-Luc plays soccer during the school year.

What if you play a musical instrument? Use the expression **jouer de**:

Sophie joue de la flûte. Ses amies jouent du piano, de la guitare, et de l'harmonica.

Grammaire
Conjugation Charts for Irregular Verbs
in the Vocabulaire

> *courir* (to run): *je cours, tu cours, il/elle court, nous courons, vous courez, ils/elles courent*
>
> *écrire* (to write): *j'écris, tu écris, il/elle écrit, nous écrivons, vous écrivez, ils/elles écrivent*
>
> *faire* (to do): *je fais, tu fais, il/elle fait, nous faisons, vous faites, ils/elles font*
>
> *lire* (to read): *je lis, tu lis, il/elle lit, nous lisons, vous lisez, ils/elles lisent*
>
> *peindre* (to paint): *je peins, tu peins, il/elle peint, nous peignons, vous peignez, ils/elles peignent*
>
> *voir* (to see): *je vois, tu vois, il/elle voit, nous voyons, vous voyez, ils/elles voient*

Le temps
Talking About the Weather

Quel temps fait-il?	What's the weather?
le temps	weather
le météo	weather forecast/report

Note how we use the verb *faire* to express weather conditions:

Il fait chaud.	It's hot.
Il fait froid.	It's cold.
Il fait frais.	It's cool.
Il fait bon.	It's nice weather.
Il fait beau.	It's beautiful weather.
Il fait mauvais.	It's bad weather.
Il fait du vent.	It's windy.
Il fait du soleil.	It's sunny.
Il pleut.	It's raining.
Il neige.	It's snowing.

77

Proverbe: Didier dit

Il pleut des cordes. It's raining cats and dogs.
(Literally: It's raining ropes.)

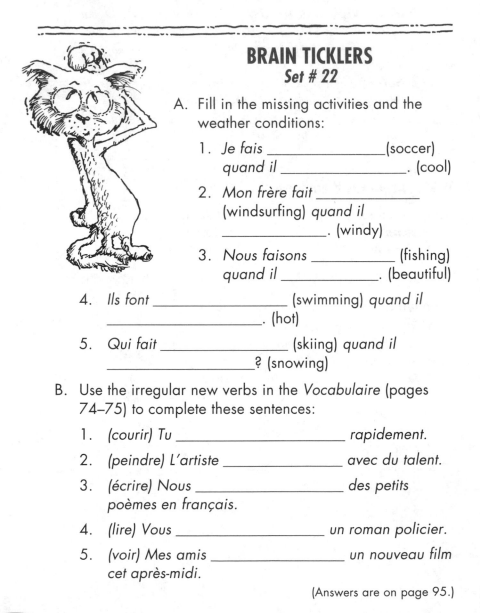

BRAIN TICKLERS
Set # 22

A. Fill in the missing activities and the weather conditions:

1. *Je fais* _____(soccer)
   quand il _____. (cool)

2. *Mon frère fait* _____
   (windsurfing) *quand il*
   _____. (windy)

3. *Nous faisons* _____ (fishing)
   quand il _____. (beautiful)

4. *Ils font* _____ (swimming) *quand il*
   _____. (hot)

5. *Qui fait* _____ (skiing) *quand il*
   _____? (snowing)

B. Use the irregular new verbs in the *Vocabulaire* (pages 74–75) to complete these sentences:

1. *(courir) Tu* _____ *rapidement.*

2. *(peindre) L'artiste* _____ *avec du talent.*

3. *(écrire) Nous* _____ *des petits poèmes en français.*

4. *(lire) Vous* _____ *un roman policier.*

5. *(voir) Mes amis* _____ *un nouveau film cet après-midi.*

(Answers are on page 95.)

Grammaire
Expressions Using Infinitives

In French, as in English, some expressions require using two verbs together, the first conjugated, the second in the **infinitive form**. The infinitive is the form that means to do something. It is the one you would find when looking up a verb in the dictionary.

> *J'aime **nager**; mon frère préfère **faire** de la planche à voile.*
> I like to swim; my brother prefers to windsurf.

Here are some verbs often followed by infinitives:

aimer	(to like)	*J'aime **lire**.* I like to read.
détester	(to hate)	*Nous détestons **faire** la vaisselle.* We hate to do the dishes.
*devoir**	(to have to)	*Je dois **faire** mes devoirs.* I have to (must) do my homework.
*espérer**	(to hope)	*Ils espèrent **gagner** le match.* They hope to win the game.
*pouvoir**	(to be able)	*Je peux **chanter** en français.* I can sing in French.
*savoir**	(to know)	*Tu sais **faire** de la photographie.* You know how to take photographs.
souhaiter	(to wish, hope)	*Elles souhaitent **voyager**.* They wish to travel.
*vouloir**	(to want)	*Vous voulez **courir** à la plage.* You want to run on the beach.

Here are the conjugations in the present tense for the preceding irregular* verbs:

devoir	(to have to):	*je dois, tu dois, il/elle doit, nous devons, vous devez, ils/elles doivent*
espérer	(to hope):	*j'espère, tu espères, il/elle espère, nous espérons, vous espérez, ils/elles espèrent*
pouvoir	(to be able):	*je peux, tu peux, il/elle peut, nous pouvons, vous pouvez, ils/elles peuvent*
savoir	(to know):	*je sais, tu sais, il/elle sait, nous savons, vous savez, ils/elles savent*
vouloir	(to want):	*je veux, tu veux, il/elle veut, nous voulons, vous voulez, ils/elles veulent*

To say these expressions in the negative, make only the first verb negative:

Nous **ne** pouvons **pas** jouer au foot avec l'équipe.
We can't play soccer with the team.
Je **ne** veux **pas** rester chez moi ce week-end.
I don't want to stay home this weekend.

However, if you want to express a **negative infinitive,** then put *ne pas* together in front of it.

Tu préfères **ne pas** perdre. You prefer not to lose.
Il espère **ne pas** marquer un but pour l'autre équipe.
He hopes he doesn't score a point for the other team.

Grammaire

The irregular verbs ***aller***, to go, and ***venir,*** to come, are used with infinitives to express the near future and the near past. Note how they are conjugated in the present indicative:

> ***aller:*** *je vais, tu vas, il/elle va, nous allons, vous allez, ils/elles vont*
>
> ***venir:*** *je viens, tu viens, il/elle vient, nous venons, vous venez, ils/elles viennent*

aller + infinitive: "going to do something" in the near future.

Je vais jouer au Monopoly avec mon frère demain soir.
I am going to play Monopoly with my brother tomorrow evening.
Vas-tu nager ce week-end?
Are you going to swim this weekend?

venir de + infinitive: to have just done something in the near past.

Marc **vient de gagner** un match de tennis.
Mark just won a tennis game.
Nous **venons d'arriver**.
We have just arrived.

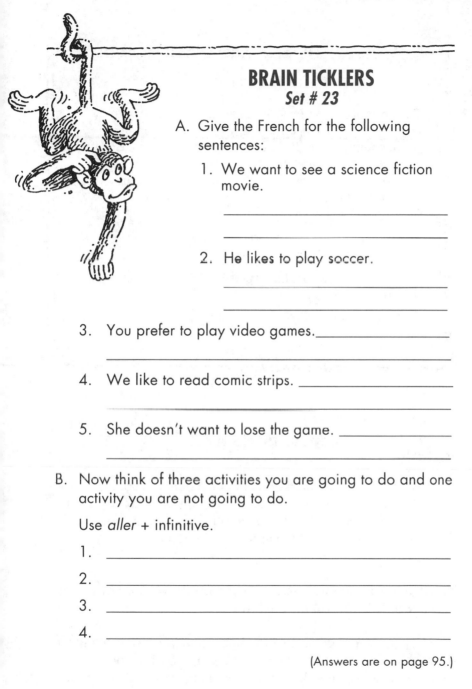

BRAIN TICKLERS
Set # 23

A. Give the French for the following sentences:

   1. We want to see a science fiction movie.

   _____

   _____

   2. He likes to play soccer.

   _____

   _____

   3. You prefer to play video games. _____

   _____

   4. We like to read comic strips. _____

   _____

   5. She doesn't want to lose the game. _____

   _____

B. Now think of three activities you are going to do and one activity you are not going to do.

   Use *aller* + infinitive.

   1. _____

   2. _____

   3. _____

   4. _____

(Answers are on page 95.)

ATTENTION!

The present perfect tense in English, conjugated with the helping verb to have, is not always the equivalent of the passé composé in French. In English, this tense is used to establish a fact: Something has happened, something has been done, but it makes no reference to specific time.

Expressions written in the passé composé that refer to time are translated as the simple past in English:

Il a acheté un vélo la semaine dernière.
He bought a bicycle last week.

But an expression that expresses a fact is translated in the present perfect:

Elle a vu le film Persepolis.
She has seen the film *Persepolis.*

Répète après moi!

When vowels precede an n or an m in French, the sound is often nasal. In this chapter, be careful to pronounce *natation* and *pla<u>n</u>che à voile* correctly. When another consonant follows the n or m or if they are the final letters of the word, the sound is nasal.

There are four basic nasal vowel sounds: *an/en* "ahn," *in* "ain," *on* "ohn," and *un* "urhn."

Keep your tongue against the bottom of your mouth and let the air hit your nasal passage. You may try holding your nose to feel and exaggerate the sound. Say these words that contain nasal vowel sounds:

an/en	in	on	un
plante	vingt	cochon (pig)	un
éléphant	cousin	font	brun
banc	pin (pine)	poisson	lundi
temps	fin	ballon	aucun

When n or m is followed by a vowel or is doubled, the nasal sound generally does *not* occur.

These vowels are *not* nasal: *d**a**me, **a**nnée, f**i**ne, b**o**nne, s**e**maine, **u**ne, aut**o**mne*.

Grammaire
Interrogative Mood: Asking Questions

There are four ways to pose a question that asks if something is so—that is, a question requiring a simple yes or no answer. For example, "Do you speak French?" can be asked in these ways:

1. ***Tu parles français?*** Use your voice to form a question by leaving the end of a statement up in the air with intonation.
2. ***Parles-tu français?*** Use inversion to switch the subject pronoun (*tu*) and the verb. (Avoid using inversion with *je*. When asking a question with *il, elle,* or *on,* add a t if the verb ends in a vowel. *Quel âge a-t-il?* How old is he?)
3. ***Est-ce que tu parles français?*** Use the phrase *est-ce que* in front of any statement to form a question.
4. ***Tu parles français, n'est-ce pas?*** Put *n'est-ce pas* at the end of a statement when you expect the responding person to agree with you. "You speak French, right?"

Did you notice that Sophie had some questions about your *loisirs,* or pastimes? Here is a list of common question words that require the speaker to give more information than just yes or no:

A quelle heure	At what time
Avec qui	With whom
Combien de	How many
Comment	How
Où	Where

Pourquoi	Why
Quand	When
Qui	Who

Use the question words with the following patterns to form information questions:

Question word + *est-ce que* + subject + verb

(Clap your hands with each part to help remind you there are four parts.)

Question word(s) (clap) *est-ce que* (clap) subject (clap) verb (clap) (repeat faster four to five times)

Où	est-ce qu'	il	joue?	Where does he play?
Comment	est-ce que	tu	danses?	How do you dance?

Question word + verb-subject

Où	joue-t-	il?	Where does he play?
Comment	danses-	tu?	How do you dance?

Qu'est-ce que "what" has *est-ce que* built in:

Qu'est-ce que tu regardes?   What are you watching?

Quel, quels (masculine) quelle, quelles (feminine):

"What" or "which" are interrogative adjectives that agree with the noun that follows:

Quelle joueuse a gagné le match? Which player won the game?

Quels spectateurs ont applaudi? Which spectators applauded?

ATTENTION!

When writing a question with **être** (to be), you write:

Question word + *être* + noun
Où est le terrain de foot? Where is the soccer field?
Qui est l'entraineur? Who is the coach?
Quel est ton sport favori? What is your favorite sport?

BRAIN TICKLERS
Set # 24

A. Match the questions on the left to the appropriate answer on the right:

1. ___ Où fais-tu de la planche à voile?

2. ___ Comment Marc joue-t-il au basket?

3. ___ Pourquoi est-ce que nous devons courir?

4. ___ Combien d'oranges veux-tu?

5. ___ Avec qui viens-tu au match?

6. ___ A quelle heure vas-tu voir le film?

7. ___ Qu'est-ce que tu écris?

a. Parce que c'est bon pour la santé

b. A huit heures

c. A la plage

d. Avec mes copains

e. Un poème d'amour

f. Pas très bien

g. Cinq, s'il te plaît

B. Complete five questions you would like to ask Sophie:

1. Où . . .

2. Comment . . .

3. Pourquoi . . .

4. Quand . . .

5. A quelle heure . . .

(Answers are on page 96.)

Vocabulaire

Encore c'est mieux

To expand your vocabulary, memorize these idiomatic expressions using the verb *faire*:

faire attention	to pay attention or watch out
faire des progrès	to make progress
faire un match	to play a game (sport)
faire partie de	to belong to
faire un voyage	to take a trip
faire la valise	to pack a suitcase
faire une faute	to make a mistake
faire le ménage	to do the housework
faire la vaisselle	to do the dishes
faire la lessive	to do the laundry
faire des courses	to go food shopping
faire le lit	to make the bed
faire du bricolage	to tinker, fix up or to do home projects
faire des achats	to go shopping

When writing a composition or a story, you can use linking words to enhance the logical progression of the story:

d'abord	first
ensuite	next
alors	so
puis	then
après	after
enfin	at last
finalement	finally

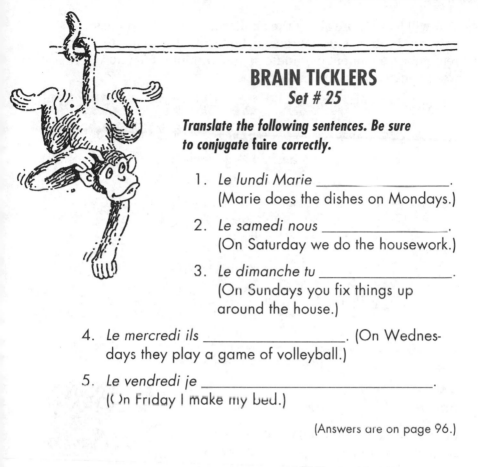

BRAIN TICKLERS
Set # 25

Translate the following sentences. Be sure to conjugate faire correctly.

1. *Le lundi Marie* _____.
   (Marie does the dishes on Mondays.)

2. *Le samedi nous* _____.
   (On Saturday we do the housework.)

3. *Le dimanche tu* _____.
   (On Sundays you fix things up around the house.)

4. *Le mercredi ils* _____. (On Wednesdays they play a game of volleyball.)

5. *Le vendredi je* _____.
   (On Friday I make my bed.)

(Answers are on page 96.)

 ## Vive la différence!

Why does ninth grade in a French school seem to be called third?

The difference is that whereas the American system counts forward (marking sixth grade as the sixth year since the child's formal education began), the French system counts backward (marking this as the sixth year until the child's secondary education will end). So in a French school, the equivalent of the American 7th grade is *cinquième* (abbreviated 5ème), 8th grade is 4ème, and so on, until 11th grade (*première*, or "first") and 12th grade, called *terminale* (or "final").

You will learn more about the similarities and differences between French and American schools in later chapters. Just remember, a student in middle school or junior high in America would be in *collège* in France.

Les écoles en France	
Schools in France	Schools in the United States
L'école maternelle (2 à 6 ans)	Nursery school and Kindergarten (2- to 6-year-olds)
L'école primaire (6 à 10 ans)	Elementary school (6- to 10-year-olds), grades 1–5
Le collège (10 à 14 ans), 6ème, 5ème, 4ème, 3ème	Middle school (10- to 14-year-olds), grades 6–9
Le lycée (15 à 18 ans), 2nd, 1ère, terminale	High school (15- to 18-year-olds), grades 10–12
L'université (18 ans...)	College and university (18+ years old)

Vocabulaire
Encore c'est mieux

French students study many of the same subjects American students do. There are a few differences. Compare the subjects on the list here to the subjects you study.

Faire is also used with the following expressions:

je fais du calcul	I study calculus
du latin	Latin
du dessin	drawing
du journalisme	journalism
des mathématiques	mathematics (*des maths*)
des sciences politiques	political science
de l'anglais	English
de l'allemand	German
de l'art	art
de l'éducation physique	physical education
de l'espagnol	Spanish
de l'histoire	history

de l'informatique	computer sciences
de la biologie	biology
de la chinoise	Chinese
de la comptabilité	accounting
de la géographie	geography
de la philosophie	philosophy
de la psychologie	psychology
de la sociologie	sociology
de la technologie	technology

Encore c'est mieux
Additional School Expressions

mon emploi du temps	my schedule
mon professeur* de français	my French teacher
ma matière préférée	my favorite subject
le/la proviseur(e)	the principal
le cours	the course
être fort/ nul(le) en . . .	to be good, strong/weak in . . .
la classe	the class
les devoirs	homework
l'ordinateur	the computer

*In France, the teachers in secondary school are called *professeurs*
In the abbreviated forms only, *un prof* or *une prof* may be used.

BRAIN TICKLERS
Set # 26

A. Answer these questions with complete
sentences.

1. *Qu'est-ce que tu fais à la maison?*

2. *Qui est ton professeur d'anglais?*

3. *Quelle est ta matière préférée?*

4. *Préfères-tu les maths ou l'histoire?*

5. *Est-ce que tu es fort en sciences?*

(Answers are on page 96.)

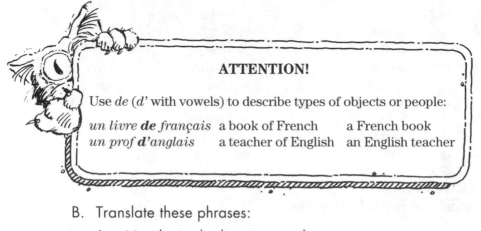

ATTENTION!

Use *de* (*d'* with vowels) to describe types of objects or people:

*un livre **de** français* a book of French a French book
*un prof **d'**anglais*   a teacher of English an English teacher

B. Translate these phrases:

1. My physical education teacher
2. Art class
3. German homework
4. My friend's schedule
5. What time is computer class?

(Answers are on page 96.)

 **Vive la différence!**

French teenagers who plan on going to university must pass a rigorous set of final exams at the end of *Terminale* called the *baccalauréat*. The *bac* includes extensive written exams, and some oral exams, in all subjects studied. There is pressure from their parents and society in general to succeed in school. The school day in France is also generally longer than in the United States and often includes classes on Saturdays; therefore, most teens do not get after-school jobs. Their job is to pass their courses and score well on their tests. This doesn't mean that students don't have fun or go out. They tend to go out in a group with *la bande de copains* and enjoy going to movies, shopping, playing video games, and attending concerts like American students. For sports and organized activities, they head for the local *Maison de Jeunes et de la Culture*, or youth center. Many sports, crafts, trips, and educational opportunities for after school and summertime are available to French teens.

A réfléchir
Le Sénégal (Senegal)

Senegal is located on the western tip of Africa. Its capital is Dakar. Its size is 76,124 square miles (197,160 km²). It is a country rich with history and culture. Senegal was once a French colony. Slavery was a part of Senegal's history before Europeans arrived in

the fifteenth century. As in many African countries, the French ruled Senegal from the middle of the seventeenth century until the mid-twentieth century. In 1960 Senegal gained its independence from France, and Leopold Senghor became president. Leopold Senghor was also a noted poet and prime participant in the independence from France. Senegal is a dynamic country made up of many ethnic groups, including the Wolof, Fulani, Tukulor, and Serere. French remains the official language. Other languages, such as Diola, Wolof, and Mandingo, are also spoken. Today the farming of peanuts, cotton, sugarcane, rice, and beans continues to be an important part of Senegal's economy. Fishing and raising livestock also add to the economy. There are many natural resources and a large variety of wildlife and birds scattered across its different game parks. The people wear colorful clothing and live in close-knit family units.

Une Carte Postale de Sénégal

Salut c'est Sophie,

Me voilà au Sénégal avec des amis de mon père. J'ai voulu visiter l'Afrique depuis toujours. Il fait chaud puisque c'est la saison sèche de novembre en juin. Après c'est la saison pluvieuse (rainy). Les enfants que j'ai

rencontrés aiment jouer au football comme en France. C'est leur passe-temps favori. Même quand ils jouent aux jeux-vidéo, ils sont des jeux de football! Mme Ndiaye porte des robes très coloriées et des turbans à la tête. Monsieur Ndiaye porte une sorte de robe qu'on appelle «un boubou» et un petit chapeau rond. Ils sont très aimables et ils veulent me montrer leur pays. Nous allons visiter un parc national: le Parc National Djoudj où je vais voir des oiseaux comme les flamants roses (flamingos), des pélicans, des cormorans, et beaucoup d'autres oiseaux migratoires. Le parc se trouve sur le fleuve Sénégal au nord de la ville de Saint Louis. Ce soir nous allons manger un plat avec des cacahouètes (peanuts), du poulet, et du riz qui s'appelle "le Mafé au poulet." C'est facile à préparer, et je vais aider Mme Ndiaye dans la cuisine.

A bientôt, Sophie

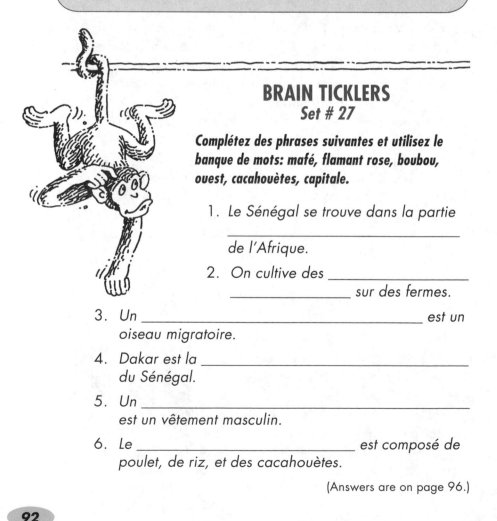

BRAIN TICKLERS
Set # 27

Complétez des phrases suivantes et utilisez le banque de mots: mafé, flamant rose, boubou, ouest, cacahouètes, capitale.

1. *Le Sénégal se trouve dans la partie* _____ *de l'Afrique.*

2. *On cultive des* _____ _____ *sur des fermes.*

3. *Un* _____ *est un oiseau migratoire.*

4. *Dakar est la* _____ *du Sénégal.*

5. *Un* _____ *est un vêtement masculin.*

6. *Le* _____ *est composé de poulet, de riz, et des cacahouètes.*

(Answers are on page 96.)

> **Tu sais quoi?**
>
> Many Americans of African descent visit l'Ile de Gorée off the coast of Dakar, Senegal, to see where slaves were held before being transported to America. Poignant pilgrimages to this historic site are educational and emotional. There are several museums of interest, including La Maison des Esclaves (The House of Slaves), built in 1776. There one can see the gate of "the trip from which no one returned" and gain an insight to the history of slavery.

Birago Diop (1906–1989), a Senegalese poet, novelist, diplomat, and veterinary surgeon, was a founder of the negritude movement in the 1930s. This movement helped promote African cultural values. Diop won the French African Grand Prix in literature in 1964. He wrote memoirs, tales, poetry, a play, and even a children's book, *Maman-Caiman*. He collected and rewrote Wolof folk tales. He was a friend of Leopold Senghor, the president of Senegal, and together they wrote *Leuk the Hare*. In his poem "*Les morts ne sont pas morts,*" he addresses the popular African belief that ancestors are present in the natural world. Here is an excerpt:

Les Morts ne Sont Pas Morts

Ecoute plus souvent
Les Choses que Les Etres
La Voix du Feu s'entend,
Entends la Voix de l'Eau.
Ecoute dans le Vent Le Buisson en sanglots:
C'est le Souffle des ancêtres.
Ceux qui sont morts ne sont jamais partis:
Ils sont dans l'Ombre qui s'éclaire
Et dans l'ombre qui s'épaissit.
Les Morts ne sont pas sous la Terre:
Ils sont dans l'Arbre qui frémit,

Ils sont dans le Bois qui gémit,
Ils sont dans l'Eau qui coule,
Ils sont dans l'Eau qui dort,
Ils sont dans la Case, ils sont dans la Foule:
Les Morts ne sont pas morts.

—Birago Diop

Vocabulaire

les choses	things
les êtres	beings/people
la voix	voice
le feu	fire
l'eau	water
le buisson	bush
en sanglots	sobbing
le souffle	breath
des ancêtres	ancestors
les morts	the dead
l'ombre	shadow
l'arbre	tree
la terre	ground
le bois	wood
la case	hut
la foule	crowd

Amis/Faux Amis

You probably noticed many *amis* among the names of sports, but here are some *faux amis* to remember:

Un but is a goal.

Le collège refers to grades 6 through 9 (sixième to troisième) in France.

Le football, le "foot" mean soccer in French.

La lecture means "reading" in French; the word for lecture is *conférence*.

Un roman is a novel, not someone from Rome.

Un mail is an email.

BRAIN TICKLERS—THE ANSWERS

Set # 22, page 78

A.
1. *du foot . . . fait frais*
2. *de la planche à voile . . . fait du vent*
3. *de la pêche . . . fait beau*
4. *de la natation . . . fait chaud*
5. *du ski . . . neige*

B.
1. *cours*
2. *peint*
3. *écrivons*
4. *lisez*
5. *voient*

Set # 23, page 81

A.
1. *Nous voulons voir un film de science fiction.*
2. *Il aime jouer au foot.*
3. *Tu préfères jouer aux jeux-vidéo.*
4. *Nous aimons lire des bandes dessinées.*
5. *Elle ne veut pas perdre le match.*

B.
Answers will vary.

Set # 24, page 85

A.
1. c
2. f
3. a
4. g
5. d
6. b
7. e

B.
Answers will vary.

Set # 25, page 87

1. *fait la vaisselle*
2. *faisons le ménage*
3. *fais du bricolage*
4. *font un match de volley*
5. *fais mon lit*

Set # 26, page 89

A.
Answers will vary.

B.
1. *mon professeur d'éducation physique*
2. *la classe d'art*
3. *les devoirs d'allemand*
4. *l'emploi du temps de mon ami(e)*
5. *À quelle heure est la classe d'informatique?*

Set # 27, page 92

1. *ouest*
2. *cacahouètes*
3. *flamant rose*
4. *capitale*
5. *boubou*
6. *mafé*

Ce que j'aime manger: La nourriture

WHAT I LIKE TO EAT: MEALS AND FOOD

*Salut! C'est Sophie. Ça va? Aujourd'hui c'est samedi. Je passe
le week-end chez mes grands-parents. Mamie, ma grand-mère,
m'amène au marché. Nous avons besoin d'acheter ce qu'il
faut pour préparer un dîner exceptionnel. Nous célébrons
l'anniversaire de Pépé, mon grand-père. En France, nous
avons de la chance parce que nous avons une variété riche
de petits magasins comme des boulangeries pour le pain, les
pâtisseries pour les desserts, et le boucher pour la viande. Bien
sûr nous pouvons aussi aller à un supermarché ou à même un
hypermarché pour tout acheter sous un toit (roof), mais pour
la qualité supérieure, nous choisissons de faire les courses
en centre ville. Nous allons aussi au marché de primeurs, des
fruits et des légumes qui s'installent le mercredi et le samedi
sur la place centrale. Mamie sélectionne de la laitue, des
tomates, des carottes, des haricots verts, et des pommes de
terre qu'elle place dans le panier (basket) qu'elle porte. Ensuite
nous trouvons des belles poires, des abricots, et des raisins.
La marchande nous invite à essayer quelques raisins. Ils sont
délicieux. A la crèmerie Mamie prend trois sortes de fromages:
du brie, du port-salut, et du chèvre. Moi, je préfère le brie. A la
boucherie M. Lebrun, le boucher, suggère un rôti du porc qu'il
pèse et emballe en papier blanc. Mamie en prend deux kilos.
Avant de rentrer à la maison, Mamie s'arrête à sa boulangerie-
pâtisserie favorite pour acheter des baguettes et un gâteau au
chocolat. Nous allons nous régaler ce soir!*

Vocabulaire

Verbes	Verbs	Verbes	Verbs
acheter	to buy	*amener*	to bring
boire	to drink	*célébrer*	to celebrate
offrir	to offer	*peser*	to weigh
placer	to place	*posséder*	to own
préférer	to prefer	*prendre*	to take or have
s'installer	to set up	*se régaler*	to feast
servir	to serve	*suggérer*	to suggest

Des magasins	Stores
la boucherie	butcher shop
(chez le boucher)	
la boulangerie	bakery
(chez le boulanger)	
la charcuterie	deli, specialty meats, prepared foods store
la crémerie	dairy store
l'épicerie (f.)	grocery store
le marché	market
le marchand	merchant
la pâtisserie	pastry shop
le hypermarché	superstore
le supermarché	supermarket

De la nourriture	Foods
un abricot/des abricots	apricot/s
une baguette	long French bread
une carotte/des carottes	carrot/s
un fromage/des fromages	cheese/s
un fruit/des fruits	fruit/s
un gâteau	cake
des haricots verts (m.)	green beans
une laitue	head of lettuce
des légumes (m.)	vegetables
un œuf	egg
un pain	loaf of bread
des pâtisseries (f.)	pastries
une poire	pear
une pomme de terre	potato

un raisin	grape
un rôti de porc	pork roast
une tomate	tomato
une viande	meat
Des quantités	**Quantities**
500 grammes	500 grams = approximately 1 pound
une boîte	box or can
une bouteille	bottle
une douzaine	dozen
un kilo	kilo = 2.2 pounds
une livre	pound
un morceau	piece
un pot	jar
un sac	bag
une tasse	cup
une tranche	slice
un verre	glass

Grammaire
The Partitive

Did you notice that Sophie said *du brie*, and *de la laitue*? These articles are called partitive articles, and they are used to express an undetermined quantity, or  "some" of something. In English we often refer to things in general without using an article; for example, we can simply say, "I'm having fruit and cheese." However, this is not the case in French: The concept of "some" must be expressed.

Partitive articles are formed with ***de* + the definite articles, *le, la, l'***. In these situations you are having a "part" of a whole, or "some" of something:

du fromage	some cheese
de la glace	some ice cream
de l'eau	some water

If the foods are countable, or you can eat one whole item such as a sandwich, then use the indefinite articles for "one," "a," or "an":

un sandwich	a/one sandwich
une pomme	an/one apple

Note that **des**, the plural form of the indefinite *de* + *les*, is the partitive plural:

des fraises	some strawberries
des frites	(some) French fries

The **partitive** and **indefinite articles** are commonly used in situations when you are talking about food: *acheter,* to buy; *avoir,* to have; *boire,* to drink; *commander,* to order; and *prendre,* to take, have (something to eat). These articles are also used with the expression *il y a,* meaning "there is" or "there are":

Je prends des cérises.	I'm having cherries.
Tu achètes une baguette.	You are buying a loaf of French bread.
Il y a des tomates sur la table.	There are some tomatoes on the table.

With the **negative,** use **de or d'** alone to express "none" or "not any":

Il n'y a pas d'abricots.	There aren't any apricots.
Ils ne prennent pas de café.	They are not having any coffee.
Nous n'avons pas de fromage.	We don't have any cheese.

ATTENTION!

There is an exception to the preceding rule: When using *être*, the "*pas de*" rule does not apply:

Ce n'est pas un citron, c'est un citron vert! That's not a lemon, it's a lime!
Ce ne sont pas des pêches. Those aren't peaches.

Use the definite articles *le, la, l'*, or *les* when you talk about foods in a more general sense, with verbs such as *aimer*, to like; *détester*, to hate; and *préférer*, to prefer; they are also used when you begin a sentence about foods:

J'aime le poulet.	I like chicken.
La pomme est excellente.	The apple is excellent.
Mon père préfère l'eau.	My father prefers water.
Les oranges sont des fruits.	Oranges are fruit.

Hint: If you can substitute the word "all," then *le, la, l', les*, the definite articles, are appropriate. *J'aime la glace.* I like **all** ice cream. *Les oranges sont des fruits.* **All** oranges are (some) fruit.

Encore c'est mieux

Use *de* in expressions of quantity:
Sophie's Mamie bought 2 *kilos* of pork. The metric system is used for measurement throughout Europe and in many countries around the world. One kilo equals 2.2 pounds. When talking about quantities, use *de* alone before the noun.

Quantities

un kilo de *carottes*	a kilo of carrots
une livre *d'abricots*	a pound of apricots
une tasse de *thé*	a cup of tea
un morceau de *fromage*	a piece of cheese

Proverbe: Didier dit

A chacun son gout. Everyone to his own taste.

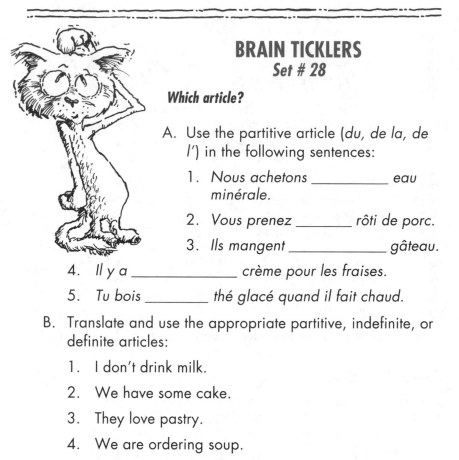

BRAIN TICKLERS
Set # 28

Which article?

A. Use the partitive article (*du, de la, de l'*) in the following sentences:

1. *Nous achetons _____ eau minérale.*

2. *Vous prenez _____ rôti de porc.*

3. *Ils mangent _____ gâteau.*

4. *Il y a _____ crème pour les fraises.*

5. *Tu bois _____ thé glacé quand il fait chaud.*

B. Translate and use the appropriate partitive, indefinite, or definite articles:

1. I don't drink milk.

2. We have some cake.

3. They love pastry.

4. We are ordering soup.

5. She likes mineral water.

6. You prefer tea.

C. Give the quantity to complete the following sentences. Make sure to use *de* or *d'*:

1. *Nous voulons _____.* (cups of coffee)

2. *Mon père achète trois _____.* (slices of ham)

3. *Pépé boit* _____. (a glass of iced tea)

4. *Le prof apporte* _____. (a bag of oranges)

5. *Il y a* _____. (a dozen eggs)

(Answers are on page 123.)

Tell me what you eat, and I will tell you what you are.

—*Brillat-Savarin*

Anthelem Brillat-Savarin (1755–1826) was an economist and lawyer, who also served for a time as mayor of Belley, the city in southern France where he was born. He is best known, however, as the author of *La Physiologie de Goût,* a treatise on *gastronomie,* or the art and science of eating well.

Brillat-Savarin's work is presented as a series of *meditations,* and these range from reflections on the sense of taste itself (the physiology), to food in general, the history and special properties of specific ingredients, on cooking and restaurants, even on sleep, dreams, obesity, and thinness.

First published in 1825, Brillat-Savarin's witty and "tasty" discourse on the pleasures and importance of good food was a great success. His aphorisms are widely quoted and considered classics in French literature. *The Physiology of Taste* was translated into English in 1949 by one of America's finest writers on food, M.F.K. Fisher, and it is still available.

Vocabulaire	
gastronome	one who is knowledgeable in *gastronomie*
gastronomie	the art and science of eating well
gourmet	also refers to one who is devoted to the enjoyment of fine food and is very knowledgeable
gourmand	one who appreciates fine food but does not necessarily have great expertise
gourmandise	the pleasure and appreciation of eating well

Grammaire
Des verbes au changement de radical
(Stem Change Verbs)

Remember that to find the stem of an *-er* verb, we simply drop the *-er* from the infinitive form. However, certain *-er* verbs are considered **stem change verbs.** As these verbs are conjugated, there are changes in the spelling of the stem. Five categories of stem change verbs are illustrated here, and most follow a "boot" pattern. That is, the forms in the boot follow a different spelling pattern from the infinitive:

```
Je
Tu
Il     Ils
Elle   Elles
```

Acheter, amener, and *peser* add an *accent grave* to the final e of the stem.

Acheter

j'achète	*nous achetons**
tu achètes	*vous achetez**
il achète	*ils achètent*
elle achète	*elles achètent*

With *préférer, suggérer, posséder,* and *célébrer,* the *accent aigu* on the final e of the stem changes to an *accent grave*:

je préfère	*nous préférons**
tu préfères	*vous préférez**
il préfère	*ils préfèrent*
elle préfère	*elles préfèrent*

With *-yer* verbs such as *nettoyer,* to clean; *employer,* to use; *essuyer,* to wipe; *essayer,* to try; and *payer,* to pay, you change the y to an i.

j'essaie	*nous essayons**
tu essaies	*vous essayez**
il essaie	*ils essaient*
elle essaie	*elles essaient*

A few verbs double the consonant before the ending. You've already seen *s'appeler* (to be called): Je m'appelle. *Jeter* (to throw) also follows the boot pattern, with a double consonant in the boot.

j'appelle	*nous appelons**
tu appelles	*vous appelez**
il appelle	*ils appellent*
elle appelle	*elles appellent*

*Attention: Note that the *nous* and *vous* forms follow the infinitive.

The last type are not boot verbs in the present tense (but will be in the imperfect tense*). They are the *-cer* and *-ger* verbs. With **-cer** verbs, to maintain the soft -c sound before the -o in the *nous* form *-ons*, you add an *accent cédille* to the c (ç) *nous commençons*, we begin.

Other *-cer* verbs that follow this pattern are *annoncer*, to announce; *prononcer*, to pronounce; *lancer*, to throw, thrust, launch; and *placer*, to place.

je commence	*nous **commençons***
tu commences	*vous commencez*
il/elle commence	*ils/elles commencent*

With **-ger** verbs, an *e* is added to the stem before the *-ons* ending. Some additional *-ger* verbs are *manger*, to eat; *voyager*, to travel; *nager*, to swim; and *ranger*, to straighten up.

je mange	***nous mangeons***
tu manges	*vous mangez*
il/elle mange	*ils/elles mangent*

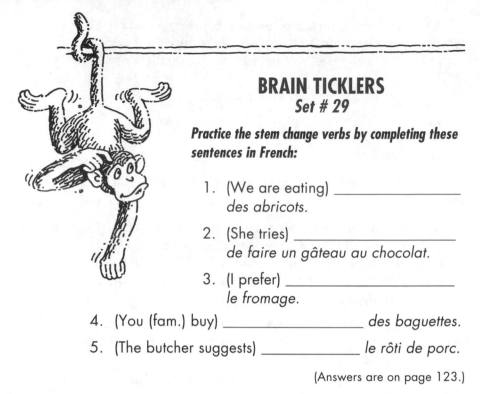

BRAIN TICKLERS
Set # 29

Practice the stem change verbs by completing these sentences in French:

1. (We are eating) _____
des abricots.

2. (She tries) _____
de faire un gâteau au chocolat.

3. (I prefer) _____
le fromage.

4. (You (fam.) buy) _____ des baguettes.

5. (The butcher suggests) _____ le rôti de porc.

(Answers are on page 123.)

Info
A Brief History of the French Restaurant

Since early in the nineteenth century, France has been associated with fine food and *gastronomie*, the cultivated knowledge and appreciation of eating well. It is no surprise, then, that the "restaurant" was invented in Paris.

The word *restaurant* comes from the verb *restaurer*, meaning to restore, fortify, bring back to good health. (And it is the same verb we use in speaking of the restoration of old buildings or paintings!) The first establishments to develop into what we know as a restaurant appeared in Paris in the 1760s. These were places that served strong broths, or *bouillons*, offered to fortify health and well-being. Over time, these restaurants began to offer customers a list, or *carte*, of offerings from which to choose. These establishments differed from traditional inns, where guests took their meal at a common table and ate whatever the innkeeper had to offer. A *restaurant*, in contrast, offered a place that was both public and private: Customers sat at individual tables yet were in a public place and could be seen partaking of these healthy broths. In fact, it was considered a sign of sophistication and refinement to be seen sipping broth rather than eating whatever crude hard-to-digest meals a peasant or simple worker might eat. Proprietors of restaurants are still called *restaurateurs* or *restauratrices*. In English this term sometimes becomes "restauranteur."

Restaurants also flourished in Paris after the revolution because the great chefs who had served royalty and the aristocracy were without employment and began to offer their skills to a wider, more democratic populace. By the 1820s, France's reputation as a place to find good food was well established and attracted travelers from America in particular. In contrast to the simple, unrefined meals Americans were accustomed to, in France travelers discovered the pleasures of eating more slowly and dining on carefully prepared food with one course following another. Today, French cuisine is enjoyed worldwide, and French wines, cheeses, and other foods can be found internationally.

Pour en savoir plus

If you would like to know more about this fascinating history, see Rebecca Spang, *The Invention of the Restaurant: Paris and Modern Gastronomic Culture* (Harvard University Press, 2000).

 Répète après moi!

As you learn more French, certain sounds will get easier for you and spelling pattern changes will become more obvious. As you saw in the stem change section, spelling changes occurred to preserve the soft c and g.

Both consonants -c and -g have hard sounds next to a, o, and u:

A *cahier* (**ka eeay**) notebook *galet* (**ga lay**) pebble
O *colle* (**kuhl**) glue *gomme* (**gum**) eraser
U *cuisine* (**kwee-zeen**) kitchen *guêpe* (**gepp**) wasp

They have soft sounds next to e and i:

E *ceci* (**ce see**) this *géant* (**jay ant**) giant
I *cil* (**seal**) eyelash *gigot* (**jee go**) leg of lamb

Grammaire

The verbs *prendre*, to have, take, choose; and *boire*, to drink, are *irregular verbs*. *Prendre* is especially useful when you are shopping for food or ordering in a restaurant. For example, *prendre un café* means "to have a coffee." Study their conjugations:

Prendre to take/to have		**Boire** to drink	
Je prends	*Nous prenons*	*Je bois*	*Nous buvons*
Tu prends	*Vous prenez*	*Tu bois*	*Vous buvez*
Il/Elle prend	*Ils/Elles prennent*	*Il/Elle boit*	*Ils/Elles boivent*

Apprendre, to learn; and *comprendre*, to understand, follow the same pattern as *prendre*.

Servir to serve

Je sers	*Nous servons*
Tu sers	*Vous servez*
Il/Elle sert	*Ils/Elles servent*

Dormir, to sleep; *partir*, to leave; and *sortir*, to go out, follow the same pattern as *servir*.

Offrir to offer

J'offre	*Nous offrons*
Tu offres	*Vous offrez*
Il/Elle offre	*Ils/Elles offrent*

Ouvrir, to open; *couvrir*, to cover; and *découvrir*, to discover follow the same pattern as *offrir*.

C'est curieux!

The word *boire* is found in the word for tip: *un pourboire*. Originally a drink was offered for a job well done. Eventually money was offered for a worker to have a drink on the tipper. Thus *un pourboire* literally means "in order to (go for a) drink."

Info

The meals in France are called *le petit déjeuner*, breakfast; *le déjeuner*, lunch; *le goûter*, snack; and *le dîner*, dinner. In French we say *prendre le petit déjeuner*, to have breakfast, but *déjeuner*, to eat lunch, and *dîner*, to eat dinner, are -er verbs. *Goûter* means to taste or to have a snack, which is very popular in France because dinner may not be until 8 PM. A favorite snack in Paris is a warm *crêpe* with your choice of fillings. Nutella is a very popular chocolate hazelnut spread that you can find in American supermarkets and try on a croissant or a piece of French bread to have a chocolate sandwich!

Vocabulaire: Encore c'est mieux

Des fruits	Fruits
un ananas	pineapple
une cerise	cherry
un citron	lemon
un citron vert	lime
une fraise	strawberry
une framboise	raspberry
une mangue	mango
une myrtille	blueberry
une orange	orange
une pastèque	watermelon
une pêche	peach
une pomme	apple

Des légumes	Vegetables
une aubergine	eggplant
une betterave	beet
un céleri	celery
un champignon	mushroom
un concombre	cucumber
une courgette	zucchini squash

des épinards (m.)	spinach
un haricot vert	green bean
un oignon	onion
un petit pois	pea
un poireau	leek
un poivron	pepper
un radis	radish

Des viandes — Meats

de l'agneau	lamb
du bœuf haché	chopped meat (ground beef)
un dindon	turkey
du jambon	ham
du porc	pork
du poulet	chicken
du rosbif	roast beef
du veau	veal

Du poisson — Fish

du saumon	salmon
de la sole	sole
du thon	tuna
une truite	trout

Des desserts — Desserts

une crème brûlée	crème brûlée
une crème caramel	caramel custard
une crêpe	French-style pancake
un éclair au chocolat	chocolate eclair
une glace	ice cream
de la mousse au chocolat	chocolate mousse
un petit gâteau	cookie
une tarte	pie

Des boissons	Drinks
un café	coffee
un chocolat	hot chocolate
un citron pressé	lemonade
de l'eau	water
de l'eau minérale (f.)	mineral water
un jus d'orange	orange juice
du lait	milk
une limonade	lemon soda
un soda	soda
un thé	tea
un thé glacé	iced tea

Des mots miscellanées	Miscellaneous Words
de la crème	cream
de la farine	flour
du ketchup	ketchup
de la mayonnaise	mayonnaise
de la moutarde	mustard
des nouilles (f.)	noodles
un œuf	an egg
des pâtes (f.pl.)	pasta
du poivre	pepper
de la purée de pommes de terre	mashed potatoes
du riz	rice
du sel	salt
de la soupe	soup
des spaghetti	spaghetti
du sucre	sugar

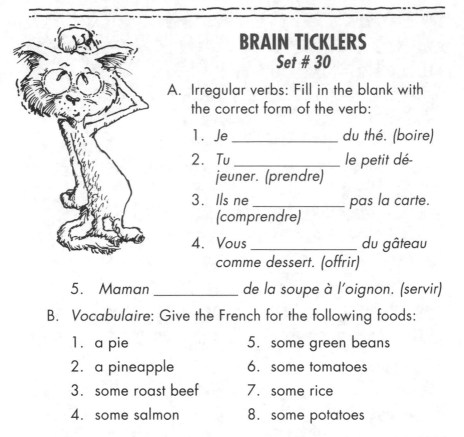

BRAIN TICKLERS
Set # 30

A. Irregular verbs: Fill in the blank with the correct form of the verb:

1. Je _____ du thé. (boire)

2. Tu _____ le petit dé-jeuner. (prendre)

3. Ils ne _____ pas la carte. (comprendre)

4. Vous _____ du gâteau comme dessert. (offrir)

5. Maman _____ de la soupe à l'oignon. (servir)

B. *Vocabulaire*: Give the French for the following foods:

1. a pie
2. a pineapple
3. some roast beef
4. some salmon
5. some green beans
6. some tomatoes
7. some rice
8. some potatoes

(Answers are on page 123.)

Tu sais quoi?

Alexandre Dumas (1802–1870), the enormously successful author of *The Three Musketeers*, *The Count of Monte Cristo*, and many other works (nearly 500!), was also known as a great cook and gastronome. In the last years of his life, he wrote *Le Grand Dictionnaire de Cuisine*; arranged alphabetically, it is a comprehensive work of history, recipes, and anecdotes. The *Dictionnaire* was published posthumously in 1873. A version of this work in English can be found in *Alexandre Dumas' Dictionary of Cuisine*, edited, abridged, and translated by Louis Colman (Simon & Schuster, 1958).

ATTENTION!

Some spelling patterns that occur in French will help you find their English meanings. For example, words that contain -ch are often words with a hard c in English: *chat*, cat; *charrette*, cart. When you see a word with an *accent circonflexe*—â, ê, î, ô, û—try adding an -s to find the English equivalent: *hôte*, *hôtesse*, host, hostess; *hâte*, haste; *tâche*, task; *dégoûtant*, disgusting. You will also often find an -s in English when you see an é: *étudiant*, student; *étable*, stable; *école*, school.

Can you guess the meaning of the following words?

Croûte: _____ *écran:* _____ *écureuil:* _____

pâte: _____ *plâtre:* _____ *honnête:* _____ *dépit:* _____

mât: _____ *hôpital:* _____ *chameau:* _____ *chapon:* _____

(crust, screen, squirrel, pasta/paste/pastry, plaster, honest, spite, mast, hospital, camel, capon)

Grammaire
Pronoms des objets directs et indirects
(Direct and Indirect Object Pronouns)

In French as in English, the action of a verb is often completed by a **direct object**, the what? or whom? that receives the action of the verb. Objects may be expressed as nouns or as pronouns.

I see my **friend**.	I see **him**.
You like **pizza**.	You like **it**.
She bought **oranges**.	She bought **them**.
We saw my **cousins**.	We saw **them**.

Direct Object Pronouns

me	me	*te*	you	*le*	him/it	*la*	her/it (*m', t', l'*)
nous	us	*vous*	you	*les*	them		

In French, these pronouns are all placed before the verb they are the objects of:

*Tu aimes **la pizza**? Oui, je **l'**aime.*
Do you like **the pizza**? Yes, I like **it**.

*Tu vas voir **le film français**? Oui, je vais **le** voir.*
Are you going to see **the French movie**? Yes, I'm going to see **it**.

In the **negative**, object pronouns stay in front of the verb, and the negative expression goes around both the verb and the object pronoun.

*Tu préfères **les oranges**? Non, je ne **les** préfère pas.*
Do you prefer **oranges**? No, I don't prefer **them**.

*Vas-tu acheter **la bouteille de soda**? Non, je ne vais pas **l'**acheter.*
Are you going to buy **the bottle of soda**? No, I'm not going to buy **it**.

*Tu **me** cherches après l'école? Non je ne **te** cherche pas.*
Are you picking **me** up after school? No, I'm not picking **you** up.

BRAIN TICKLERS
Set # 31

Use the correct direct object pronoun to answer these questions in French:

1. *Préfères-tu les cerises?* _____
   _____ Yes, I prefer them.

2. *Choisit-il la pomme rouge?*
   _____ _____ No, he's not choosing it.

3. *M'aimes-tu?* _____
   Yes, I like you.

4. *Les enfants nous écoutent?* _____
   No, they're not listening to you.

5. *Allons-nous danser le tango?* _____
   Yes, we are going to dance it.

(Answers are on page 123.)

Indirect objects refer to those who receive the action of a verb indirectly, answering the questions, **to whom? to what?**

Indirect Object Pronouns

me to me	*te* to you	*lui* to him / to her
nous to us	*vous* to you	*leur* to them

> *Tu donnes des fraises **à ta mère**? Oui, je **lui** donne des fraises.*
> Are you giving strawberries **to your mother**? Yes, I'm giving strawberries **to her**.

> *Sophie **t'**apporte une tarte? Oui, elle **m'**apporte une tarte.*
> Is Sophie bringing **you** a pie? Yes, she is bringing **me** a pie.

Note: Verbs that deal with speaking or writing **to someone** take an indirect object: *parler à*, to speak to; *dire à*, to say; *répondre à*, to answer; *poser une question à*, to ask a question; *demander à*, to ask; *écrire à*, to write to; *lire à*, to read to.

> *Nous parlons **aux voisins** des élections. Nous **leur** parlons des élections.*
> We talk **to the neighbors** about the elections. We talk **to them** about the elections.

> *Qui va répondre **au prof**? Robert va **lui** répondre.*
> Who's going to answer **the teacher**? Robert is going to answer **him**.

There are two more object pronouns: *y* and *en.*

Y replaces

- nouns that are things introduced by *à* (to + something), such as *à la lettre (to the letter)*
- prepositional phrases such as *chez moi* (at my house), *derrière l'école* (behind the school). It means **it** or **there**.

> *Réponds-tu **à la lettre**? Non, je n'**y** réponds pas.*
> Are you answering **the letter**? No, I'm not answering **it**.

> *Ta grand-mère va **au supermarché**? Oui, elle **y** va.*
> Is your grandmother going **to the supermarket**? Yes, she is going **there**.

> *Vont-ils jouer **derrière l'école**? Oui, ils vont **y** jouer.*
> Are they going to play **behind the school**? Yes, they are going to play **there**.

En replaces nouns or phrases that are introduced by forms of *de (de la, du, de l', des)* or numbers: It can mean **some** or **of them**.

As-tu ***des bananes*** pour le dessert? Oui, ***j'en*** ai.
Do you have **bananas** for dessert? Yes, I have **some**.

Combien ***de bananes*** y a-t-il? Il y **en** a six.
How many **bananas** are there? There are six **of them**.

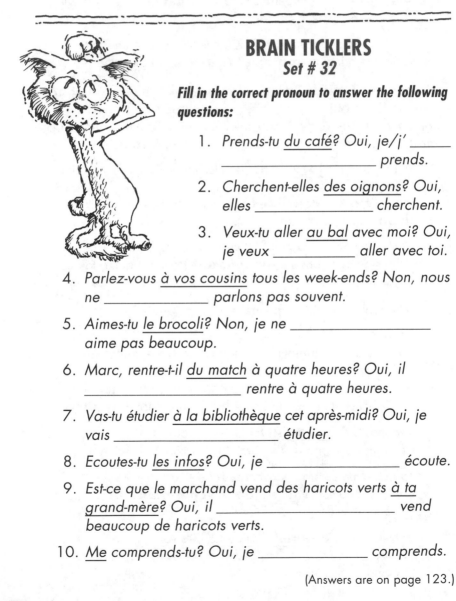

BRAIN TICKLERS
Set # 32

Fill in the correct pronoun to answer the following questions:

1. Prends-tu <u>du café</u>? Oui, je/j' _____ _____ prends.

2. Cherchent-elles <u>des oignons</u>? Oui, elles _____ cherchent.

3. Veux-tu aller <u>au bal</u> avec moi? Oui, je veux _____ aller avec toi.

4. Parlez-vous <u>à vos cousins</u> tous les week-ends? Non, nous ne _____ parlons pas souvent.

5. Aimes-tu <u>le brocoli</u>? Non, je ne _____ aime pas beaucoup.

6. Marc, rentre-t-il <u>du match</u> à quatre heures? Oui, il _____ rentre à quatre heures.

7. Vas-tu étudier <u>à la bibliothèque</u> cet après-midi? Oui, je vais _____ étudier.

8. Ecoutes-tu <u>les infos</u>? Oui, je _____ écoute.

9. Est-ce que le marchand vend des haricots verts <u>à ta grand-mère</u>? Oui, il _____ vend beaucoup de haricots verts.

10. <u>Me</u> comprends-tu? Oui, je _____ comprends.

(Answers are on page 123.)

A réfléchir
La Belgique (Belgium)

Belgium is a small country, only 6 percent of the size of France. It is located to the north of France and borders Holland, Germany, Luxembourg, and the North Sea. It is actually made up of three parts: In the north it is called the Flemish region, La Région Flamande; the capital Brussels is located in the central Brussels region, or La Région de Bruxelles; and in the south is the Walloon region, or La Région Wallonne. In the Flemish region, Flemish is spoken and the laws and government are specific to this northern region. In the Brussels and Walloon regions, French is the primary language. Belgium has a long colorful history, which includes invasions by many tribes and the Romans as well. It is known for producing delicious chocolate, not so delicious brussels sprouts, and Belgian waffles. French fries were actually invented in Belgium. Many original festivals are held throughout the year in Belgium, and thousands flock to Binche to be pelted with oranges by men wearing spooky masks and bizarre ostrich hats in celebration of Mardi Gras. In Stavelot there is a carnival on the fourth Sunday of Lent. The participants wear strange white-capped masks with long noses and are called Blancs Moussis. Adolphe Sax of Dinant, Belgium, presented his new invention, the saxophone, in 1846. The Belgians have a passion for comic strips, and large murals of favorite characters decorate the city of Brussels. Tintin by Hergé and the Smurfs by Peyo have worldwide recognition. To see images of a Blanc Moussi or Tintin, search on *google.fr* and read about them in French!

Qu'est-ce que la santé? C'est du chocolat!
What is health? It is chocolate!
—Anthelme Brillat-Savarin

Une Carte Postale de Belgique

Salut! C'est Sophie.

Notre famille fait un voyage en Belgique. Nous visitons de jolies villes comme Bruges et Bruxelles. En route nous avons mangé beaucoup de frites et de chocolat. Les Belges sont gentils, mais il faut faire attention à respecter les deux langues qu'on parle ici. Les Flamands préfèrent que nous essayons de parler un peu en flamand, et les Wallonnes insistent que nous parlons français—ce n'est pas un problème pour moi! Il y a quelques petites différences entre le français de Paris et le français de Bruxelles—par exemple quand nous disons soixante-dix, on nous corrige en disant septante, et il existe le mot nonante pour quatre-vingt-dix. Quand nous disons au revoir, ils disent «bonne journée» ou «bonne soirée» si c'est le soir! Ce que je trouve intéressant c'est qu'il y a un Roi de Belgique: Le Roi Philippe. Il s'intéresse à encourager les deux parties de la Belgique à travailler ensemble pour rester un pays fort. Le Roi Philippe est marié à La Reine Mathilde et ils ont quatre enfants. Je recommande que tu viennes visiter ce pays fascinant!

Sophie

BRAIN TICKLERS
Set # 33

Read the following statements in French and decide if they are true or false based on the information you read about Belgium in A réfléchir and Une Carte Postale.

1. _____ *Au Nord se trouve la Région Flamande.*

2. _____ *On mange beaucoup de tartes au citron en Belgique.*

3. _____ *On dit septante pour le numéro quatre-vingts.*

4. _____ Les Blancs Moussis sont des petits gâteaux à la vanille.

5. _____ Les bandes dessinées sont très populaires en Belgique.

(Answers are on page 123.)

Tu sais quoi?

A husband who was trying to please his wife and children invented French fries. Since his family loved to eat fried whiting fish in the summer, he tried to recreate a fried substitute in the wintertime. There was an abundance of potatoes in his basement, so he fried them up. His "frites" were cut to the size of the popular small fish, and his family loved them. In Belgium they are still popular and are twice fried to be extra crispy.

The Belgian rapper known as **Stromae** was born Paul Van Haver in Brussells in 1985. His mother is Flemish and his father was Rwandan. His musical style is a creative blend of electronic and hip hop. His videos, music, and style are popular worldwide, and he has won many awards for his hits, starting with "Alors on danse." He was the Belgian Breakthrough Artist of the Year in 2009. In 2015, he was awarded the Best Concert honors at the *Victoires de la Musique* show in Paris, given by the French prime minister. He continues to write music and tour worldwide. Stromae has a unique flair for style, and even has his own fashion label, Mosaert—an anagram of his name.

Amis/Faux Amis

Le four is the oven in French.　　　*Un raisin* is a grape.
Un pot means a jar, not a cooking pot.　　*Le pain* is the bread.

Un menu in France refers to a meal at a fixed price, or *prix fixe*. To see a menu in a French restaurant, ask for *la carte*.

But there are many *amis* among the names of foods:

un abricot (apricot)	*une tomate*	*une carotte*
une pâtisserie (pastry)	*une poire* (pear)	*un fruit, des fruits*

A final word from Brillat-Savarin:

On peut tout faire avec des mayonnaises, sauf s'asseoir dessus.
One can do everything with a mayonnaise, except sit on it!

BRAIN TICKLERS—THE ANSWERS

Set # 28, page 104

A.
1. *de l'*
2. *du*
3. *du*
4. *de la*
5. *du*

B.
1. *Je ne bois pas de lait.*
2. *Nous avons du gâteau.*
3. *Ils adorent les pâtisseries.*
4. *Nous commandons de la soupe.*
5. *Elle aime l'eau minérale.*
6. *Tu préfères le thé.*

C.
1. *des tasses de café*
2. *tranches de jambon*
3. *un verre de thé glacé*
4. *un sac d'oranges*
5. *une douzaine d'œufs*

Set # 29, page 108

1. *Nous mangeons*
2. *Elle essaie*
3. *Je préfère*
4. *Tu achètes*
5. *Le boucher suggère*

Set # 30, page 114

A.
1. *bois*
2. *prends*
3. *comprennent*
4. *offrez*
5. *sert*

B.
1. *une tarte*
2. *un ananas*
3. *du rosbif*
4. *du saumon*
5. *des haricots verts*
6. *des tomates*
7. *du riz*
8. *des pommes de terre*

Set # 31, page 116

1. *Oui, je les préfère.*
2. *Non, il ne la choisit pas.*
3. *Oui, je t'aime.*
4. *Non, ils ne vous écoutent pas.*
5. *Oui, nous allons le danser.*

Set # 32, page 118

1. *en*
2. *en*
3. *y*
4. *leur*
5. *l'*
6. *en*
7. *y*
8. *les*
9. *lui*
10. *te*

Set # 33, page 120

1. *vrai*
2. *faux*
3. *faux*
4. *faux*
5. *vrai*

Ce que j'aime porter: Les vêtements

WHAT I LIKE TO WEAR: CLOTHING

Bonjour! Ça va? Moi, ça va bien. Ce soir je suis en train de faire du baby-sitting. Je garde Marie, l'enfant de nos voisins, les Lefèvre. Marie a six ans, et je la trouve très coquette (concerned with her appearance). Elle aime jouer à être actrice et s'habiller comme une star! Moi, à son age j'étais beaucoup moins coquette: je m'habillais en jean avec un tee-shirt décoloré et des vieux tennis confortables! Ce soir Marie s'habille dans une jupe rouge de velours avec un joli chemisier de soie blanche. Elle a cherché dans le placard de sa mère et a trouvé un foulard et des chaussures à talons hauts. Je ne me rendais pas compte qu'elle se mettait aussi le maquillage de sa mère qu'elle a trouvé dans la salle de bains. Elle se maquille de mascara aux cils et du rouge à lèvres aux lèvres (lips). Imagine ma surprise quand elle entre dans le salon et trottine de long en large (up and down) sur le tapis. Je lui permets de jouer jusqu'à huit heures, l'heure de se coucher. Alors je lui demande de se déshabiller et de mettre son pyjama en flanelle rose. Elle proteste un peu quand je lui demande de se démaquiller bien et de se laver la figure. Ensuite elle se brosse les dents et les cheveux et saute dans son lit. Marie se couche et je lui lis l'histoire de Cendrillon (Cinderella), une édition avec de belles images. Marie adore regarder les robes de soirée élégantes au bal du Prince Charmant. Le prince porte un costume extraordinaire de velours bleu marine avec une chemise décorée de dentelle blanche. Enfin Marie s'endort pour rêver du prince et je me lève silencieusement pour descendre au salon. Je me regarde dans le miroir et je me trouve assez belle mais un peu fatiguée! Je m'assieds devant l'ordinateur pour regarder les catalogues en ligne de vêtements. Je dois trouver une robe pour le mariage de mon cousin le mois prochain. Il se peut que j'y rencontre un prince charmant moderne.

Vocabulaire

Les vêtements	Clothing
un anorak	parka
un blouson	jacket
des bottes (f.)	boots

une casquette	cap
un chapeau	hat
un foulard	scarf
des gants (m.)	gloves
un imperméable	raincoat
un jean	jeans
un legging	leggings
un pull-over (un pull)	sweater
un pyjama	pajamas
une robe	dress
des tennis (f.)	sneakers
des chaussettes (f.)	socks
des chaussures (f.)	shoes
une chemise	shirt (for man)
un chemisier	blouse
un costume	suit (for man)
une jupe	skirt
un maillot de bain	bathing suit
un manteau	overcoat
un pantalon	pants
des sandales (f.)	sandals
un short	shorts
un sweat-shirt	sweatshirt
des sous-vêtements (m.)	underwear
un tee-shirt	T-shirt
un débardeur	tank top
Les matériaux	**Materials**
le coton	cotton
le cuir	leather

le daim	suede
la dentelle	lace
la flanelle	flannel
le laine	wool
la soie	silk
le velours	velvet
à carreaux	checkered
à pois	polka dotted
uni	solid
fleuri	flowered
rayé	striped
des rayures	stripes
du parfum	perfume
Miscellanées	**Miscellaneous Expressions**
assez beau	rather beautiful
à la mode	In style
BCBG	preppy
bon marché	inexpensive
branché	in style, hip
cher (chère)	expensive
chic	stylish
court	short
criard	loud
décoloré	faded
démodé	out of style
génial	awesome
large	baggy
moche	ugly
pas assez grand	not big enough

serré	tight
taille moyenne	average size
trop grand	too big
trop petit	too small

Use *de* for the type of material: *un jean de coton*

mettre	to put on
porter	to wear

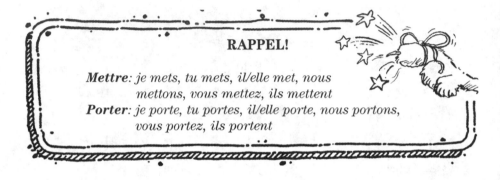

RAPPEL!

Mettre: *je mets, tu mets, il/elle met, nous mettons, vous mettez, ils mettent*
Porter: *je porte, tu portes, il/elle porte, nous portons, vous portez, ils portent*

BRAIN TICKLERS
Set # 34

Write the following expressions in French:

1. His pants are too (*trop*) baggy.

2. The sweater is an average size.

3. We put on leather boots.

4. She is wearing a blue polka-dot dress.

5. He prefers to wear faded blue jeans.

(Answers are on page 147.)

Grammaire
Reflexive Verbs

In English when we talk about our daily routine and ourselves, we often say, "I get dressed" (I dress myself) or "I bathe" (I wash myself). In French such verbs are considered reflexive. You can tell if a verb is reflexive when you see *se*, the reflexive pronoun that means "oneself." In Chapter 1 you learned the expression, *je m'appelle* . . . , which means "I am called . . ." or "My name is . . . ." *S'appeler* is a reflexive verb.

To make it easier to understand, we'll say "yourself" as we translate. The pronouns follow this pattern:

me	*nous*
te	*vous*
se	*se*

Here are the conjugations for *se laver* and *s'habiller*:

je me lave	*je m'habille*
tu te laves	*tu t'habilles*
il se lave	*il s'habille*
elle se lave	*elle s'habille*
nous nous lavons	*nous nous habillons*
vous vous lavez	*vous vous habillez*
ils se lavent	*ils s'habillent*
elles se lavent	*elles s'habillent*

Negative: *Je ne me lave pas avant un match de foot.* I don't bathe before a soccer game.

Interrogative: *Est-ce que tu te laves souvent les mains?* Do you wash your hands often?

Inversion: *Te laves-tu le matin ou le soir?* Do you bathe in the morning or in the evening?

Negative inversion: *Ne te laves-tu pas après un match de foot?* Don't you bathe after a soccer game?

When there is an **infinitive** construction, the pronoun reflects the original subject of the verb:

*Tu vas **te coucher** à 10h.* You are going to go to bed at 10 o'clock.

*Nous **n'**allons **pas nous lever** tôt.* We aren't going to get up early.

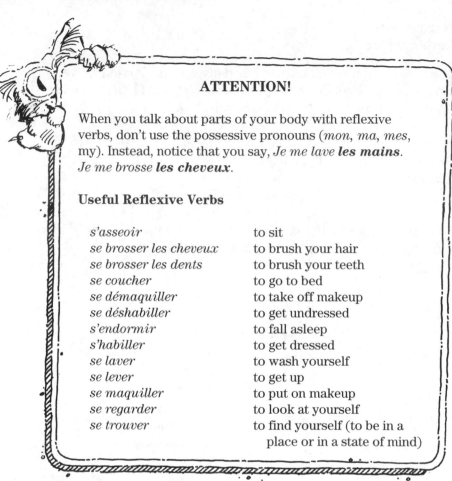

ATTENTION!

When you talk about parts of your body with reflexive verbs, don't use the possessive pronouns (*mon, ma, mes,* my). Instead, notice that you say, *Je me lave **les mains**. Je me brosse **les cheveux**.*

Useful Reflexive Verbs

s'asseoir	to sit
se brosser les cheveux	to brush your hair
se brosser les dents	to brush your teeth
se coucher	to go to bed
se démaquiller	to take off makeup
se déshabiller	to get undressed
s'endormir	to fall asleep
s'habiller	to get dressed
se laver	to wash yourself
se lever	to get up
se maquiller	to put on makeup
se regarder	to look at yourself
se trouver	to find yourself (to be in a place or in a state of mind)

Proverbe: Didier dit

Qui se ressemble s'assemble. Birds of a feather flock together. (Literally: Those who are alike gather together.)

BRAIN TICKLERS
Set # 35

Translate the following:

1. We go to bed at 10:30 in the evening.

2. They get up at 7 o'clock in the morning.

3. She is putting on her makeup.

4. They are getting undressed now (*maintenant*).

5. You are falling asleep. (fam.)

(Answers are on page 147.)

Info
French Fashion and Style

Since the days of the extravagant court under Louis XIV (1638–1715), France has represented elegance, luxury, and style in fashion. What is now known as *haute couture*, or literally, "high sewing," actually began in Paris with the House of Worth, founded in 1858 by an Englishman named Charles Frédéric Worth. Worth's creations were designed for individual clients and represented the finest in materials and perfection in fitting, sewing, and tailoring.

The designation *haute couture* is a term protected by French law: to be categorized *haute couture*, the fashion house must adhere to certain guidelines, which include the obligation to present new collections in the spring and the fall of at least thirty-five items for review by the press and eager potential clients.

There are many designers and fashion houses throughout the world now, but there are only ten houses of fashion in France that retain the official designation of *haute couture*. These include Dior, Givenchy, and Chanel. Beginning with the House of Worth, the *couturiers* also began to offer jewelry and other accessories under their names, but in the 1920s it was Coco Chanel who first introduced perfume—her famous "Number 5"—as a *couturier* item.

Grammaire
Adjectifs interrogatifs et démonstratifs

Interrogative and Demonstrative Adjectives: *Quel* and *Ce*

Interrogative adjectives: *Quels* vêtements préfères-tu? What type of clothes do you prefer? ***Quel*** means what or which, and like other adjectives must agree with the noun it modifies:

	Singular	Plural
Masculine:	*quel*	*quels*
Feminine:	*quelle*	*quelles*

Quel pantalon va avec cette chemise?	What pants go with this shirt?
Quelle robe choisis-tu?	Which dress are you choosing?
Quelles chaussures sont en solde?	Which shoes are on sale?
Quels vêtements prends-tu en vacances?	Which clothes are you taking on vacation?

Demonstrative adjectives follow a different pattern. *Ce* means this or these:

	Singular	Plural
Masculine	*ce*	
Masculine vowel	*cet*	*ces*
Feminine	*cette*	

Cet is the form used before masculine nouns beginning with a vowel or silent -h:

cet anorak

Note that in the plural you say *ces anoraks*. *Ces* is used before masculine and feminine plurals.

> ***Ces*** sandales sont trop grandes. These sandals are too big.
> ***Ce*** soir je vais mettre ***ce*** pull en laine. Tonight I am going to put on this woolen sweater.

To add emphasis when comparing items, add *-ci* for this and *-là* for there:

> ***Cette*** robe-***ci*** est plus jolie que ***cette*** robe-***là***.
> This dress is prettier than that one.

Ces *gants-**ci** sont moins chers que **ces** gants-**là**.*
These gloves are less expensive than those gloves.

ATTENTION!

Note that *-ci* and *-là* are always attached by a hyphen to the noun they follow.

BRAIN TICKLERS
Set # 36

A Fill in first the interrogative adjectives and second the demonstrative adjectives:

1. _____ *blouson aimes-tu? J'aime* _____ *blouson en cuir marron.*

2. _____ *sandales vas-tu porter? Je vais porter* _____ *sandales rouges.*

3. _____ *robe met-elle? Elle met* _____ *robe de coton rouge.*

4. _____ *chaussettes achètes-tu? J'achète* _____ *chaussettes noires.*

5. _____ *imper préfères-tu? Je préfère* _____ *imper à rayures bleue.*

B. Translate these sentences. Remember to add *–ci* or *–là* when contrasting this and that:

1. Do you like this T-shirt or that T-shirt?

2. Who is buying this red sweater?

3. My father likes this blue parka, but I prefer that black parka.

4. Are you buying these woolen socks or those cotton socks?

(Answers are on page 147.)

Grammaire
La comparaison et la superlative
(Comparisons and Superlatives)

Did you notice that Sophie said she was less *coquette* than Marie? *Je suis beaucoup moins coquette que Marie.* You may know that Cinderella was the most beautiful girl at the ball *Cendrillon était la plus belle fille du bal.* These constructions are formed by adding comparative and superlative words.

Comparative: Add the words (more) ***plus***, (less) ***moins***, (as) ***aussi***, in front of the adjective, and **que** (than) in front of the second part of the comparative phrase:

> *Jean-Pierre est **plus** grand **que** Sophie.*
> Jean-Pierre is taller than Sophie.

> *Sophie est **moins** grande **que** Jean-Pierre.*
> Sophie is less tall than Jean-Pierre.

> *Robert est **aussi** grand **que** Jean-Pierre.*
> Robert is as tall as Jean-Pierre.

Notice that the adjective agrees with the first noun. Sophie, *grande*; Robert, *grand*.
   One exception is the word ***bon.*** It changes to ***meilleur,*** just like "good" changes to "better" in English.

> *M. Rimbaud est un **bon** vendeur, mais M. Verlaine est un **meilleur** vendeur.*
> Mr. Rimbaud is a good salesman, but Mr. Verlaine is a better salesman.

Superlative: To form the superlative, add **le/la/les** (the) in front of **plus, moins,** or **meilleur,** and **de** before the group that represents the second element:

> *C'est **la plus** jolie jupe **du** magasin.* That's the prettiest skirt in the store.
> *C'est le pantalon **le moins** cher **de la** boutique.* That's the least expensive pair of pants in the boutique.
> *C'est la chemise **la plus** criard **du** rayon.* It's the loudest shirt in the department.
> *C'est **la meilleure** prix **de la** saison.* It's the best price of the season.

RAPPEL!

If the adjective is a BAGS (beauty, age, goodness, size) adjective, it is placed in front of the noun along with the superlative constructions: "*C'est la plus jolie robe.*" *Beau, joli, jeune, nouveau, vieux, bon, mauvais, petit, grand, gros, long,* and *large* all follow that pattern.

Most other adjectives follow the noun: *la chemise la plus criard. La plus criard*, the loudest, follows the noun.

BRAIN TICKLERS
Set # 37

A. Compare your clothes to your friend's clothes:

1. *Mon jean est _____ _____ nouveau que son jean.* (newer)

2. *Mon pullover est _____ _____ BCBG que son pull-over.* (less preppy)

3. *Mes tennis sont _____ confortables.* (as comfortable)

4. *Ma casquette est _____ chic que sa casquette.* (more classy)

B. Translate these phrases:

1. The prettiest evening gown
2. The ugliest hat
3. The best bathing suit
4. The funniest pajamas
5. The oldest shoes
6. The coolest jacket

(Answers are on page 148.)

Vocabulaire: Encore c'est mieux

La toilette

Encore des verbes réflexives

se coiffer	to style your hair
se couper	to cut yourself
se peigner	to comb your hair
se préparer	to get ready
se promener	to take a walk
se raser	to shave
se regarder	to look at yourself
se sécher	to dry yourself

D'autres verbes reflexives

s'amuser	to have a good time
s'attendre à	to expect
se dépêcher	to hurry
s'ennuyer	to get bored
s'excuser	to apologize
s'inquiéter	to worry
se moquer de	to mock
se sentir	to feel
se souvenir	to remember
se taire	to be quiet

Encore de parties du corps — More Parts of the Body

Cheveux — Hair

une frange	bangs
frisés	curly

une natte	braid
une queue de cheval	ponytail
raids/lisses	straight
une raie	part (in hair)

Le visage — Face

un œil (sing.) les yeux (pl.)	eye/eyes
un cil	eyelash
un front	forehead
une joue	cheek
une lèvre	lip
un menton	chin
un sourcil	eyebrow

Miscellanées — Miscellaneous

une aisselle	armpit
un lobe de l'oreille	earlobe
un nombril	belly button; navel
un ongle	nail

Des bijoux et des accessoires — Jewelry and Accessories

une bague	ring
une boucle d'oreille	earring
une ceinture	belt
une chaîne	chain
un collier	necklace
une cravate	tie
des écouteurs	earbuds
une montre	watch

RAPPEL!

Remember that verbs are considered reflexive when the action is "reflected" back to the subject. Note the actions of the verbs in the preceding list. These are things you do to or for yourself. When you see a verb listed with *s'* or *se*, it means that you must use the subject pronoun *and* the reflexive pronoun when you conjugate it.

BRAIN TICKLERS
Set # 38

A. Form sentences with these elements. Be sure to conjugate the verbs correctly.

1. *Je / s'habiller / en jean blanc*
2. *Tu / se maquiller / avec du mascara*
3. *Ils / se raser / la figure*
4. *Mes parents / ne pas / se coucher / à neuf heures*
5. *Vous / aller / se promener / au parc*

B. *Détails*

Use the new vocabulary to complete these sentences:

1. *Pierre se rase avec un _____* (razor) *électrique.*
2. *Tu te laves les cheveux avec du _____.* (shampoo)
3. *Marie met du mascara aux _____.* (eyelashes)
4. *Sophie se coupe les _____* (nails) *avec des ciseaux* (scissors).
5. *Nous mettons du déodorant aux _____.* (armpits)
6. *Ma tante adore porter des _____* (earrings) *originales.*

C. Respond to the following questions with complete sentences:

1. *Te souviens-tu de ton premier professeur?*

2. *Est-ce que ton frère/ta sœur se moque de toi?*

3. *Comment est-ce que tu t'amuses après l'école?*

4. *Te peignes-tu ou te brosses-tu les cheveux le matin?*

5. *Comment te sens-tu aujourd'hui?*

(Answers are on page 148.)

Répète après moi!

The "wah" sound of the *oi* spelling is found in many words. In this chapter we've seen *soie*, silk, and *à pois*, polka dotted. You already know *trois*, *toi*, *moi*, *choisis*, and *vois*. Say these words with the "wah" sound, keeping the ah sound open as if you were at the dentist:

> *foi, loi, crois, dois, droit, bois, gaulois, noix, oiseaux, petits pois, hautbois, quoi, roi, soi, trois, vois, pourquoi*
> faith, law, believe, must, right, wood, Gaul, nuts, birds, peas, oboe, what, king, oneself, three, see, why

Grammaire
Commands with Object Pronouns and Reflexive Verbs

When you give a command, the object pronouns follow the verb and are attached with hyphens.

> *Donne-**moi*** une banane. Give me a banana.
> *Apportez-**nous** des sodas, s'il vous plaît.* Bring us sodas, please.

**Attention*: Positive Commands

Me changes to **moi**.
Te changes to **toi**.

In the negative, keep the pronoun **in front** of the verb:

> *Ne **me** téléphone pas ce soir!* Don't call me tonight!
> *Ne **lui** parlez pas en classe!* Don't talk to him in class!

The reflexive pronouns follow the same pattern:

> *Brosse-**toi** les dents avant de te coucher.* Brush your teeth before going to bed.
>
> *Levez-**vous** pour jouer à "Simon dit."* Get up to play "Simon says."
>
> *Ne **te** promène pas trop près de la rive.* Don't walk too close to the riverbank.
>
> *Ne **nous** asseyons pas sur le cactus.* Let's not sit on the cactus.

BRAIN TICKLERS
Set # 39

A. Form commands with the following elements, using the verb forms indicated in parentheses:

1. *(tu) Rendre / me / mon sac à dos.*
2. *(tu) Rencontrer / nous / devant la boutique.*
3. *(vous) Passer / nous / le dentifrice.*
4. *(vous) Apporter / me / ma veste / du placard*
5. *(vous) Prêter / nous / des gants*

B. Now pretend you are playing *Simon dit,* Simon says. Tell class members to do the following: (Remember to use reflexive verbs.)

1. Simon says: Get up!
2. Simon says: Sit down!
3. Simons says: Walk to the blackboard!
4. Simon says: Stop!
5. Simon says: Fix your hair!
6. Sit down! (and of course whoever sits down loses because Simon didn't say Simon says!)

(Answers are on page 148.)

Info
L'Histoire de Paris

The island in the center of modern Paris, called the Ile de la Cité, was first settled by a tribe known as the Parisii around 250 BC. Later conquered by the Romans and often invaded by other forces, the island served as the region's center of activity through the Middle Ages. The famous cathedral of Notre Dame, begun in 1163, is located on the Ile de la Cité, and the island remains the judicial center of Paris today. One can visit sites that date from the Middle Ages and see actual Roman ruins at the Cluny museum nearby.

The city of Paris expanded beyond the Ile de la Cité and the Ile St. Louis, to what we now know as the *rive gauche* and *rive droit*, the left and right banks of the river Seine. The traditional character of each also dates back to the 1200s—the left bank as a *quartier* for students, artists, and intellectuals, the right bank as a center for business and the central market known as les Halles. The Louvre, now the most famous museum in Paris, was originally part of the fortifications to protect the expanding city; after 1530 François I began work on the Louvre to make it a royal palace.

Over the centuries, various rulers left their mark on the growth of this great city. After the revolution, Napoléon as emperor began many *grands projets*, including l'Arc de Triomphe. But it was during the period known as the second empire that Paris became the city of grand vistas and public spaces we see today. Napoléon III gave responsibility for development of the city to Georges Haussman, and it was Haussman who had many old and densely populated sections in the city demolished. Haussman was also responsible for creating a municipal water system and the famous underground sewers of Paris. This renovation of Paris resulted in the *grands boulevards* and in thousands of acres of parks and gardens, new theaters, and hospitals. The redesign of the city had strategic value as well. The more open city with wide avenues was much easier to defend against popular uprisings!

The tradition of *grands projets* in Paris was also seen in grand expositions, or world fairs, which celebrated scientific and industrial progress. The *Tour Eiffel* was the central attraction of the 1889 exposition and was meant to last only twenty years, but it became a symbol of Paris and remains one of the most popular destinations in the city. The tradition of *grands projets* continues to this day, reflecting the desire of recent French presidents to leave their mark on the city. Some of these include the very modern art museum in the *Centre Pompidou*, the *musée d'Orsay*, *l'Arche de la Défense*, and the installation of the *pyramide* in the courtyard of the Louvre. In 2006, then-President Chirac celebrated the opening of the new *Musée du Quai Branly*, devoted entirely to non-Western art.

At the end of October 2014, after twelve years in the making, the *Fondation Louis Vuitton* opened in Paris. Designed by American architect Frank Gehry, the art museum and cultural center, sponsored by the French luxury goods brand, is a spectacular landmark in Bois de Boulogne park to the west of Paris. In addition, the Musée Picasso in Paris has reopened after being closed for a five-year renovation. Now doubled in size, the museum is able to display many of the 5,000 Picasso drawings, sculptures, photographs, and archive materials that were previously hidden from public view.

www.fondationlouisvuitton.fr/en   www.museepicassoparis.fr

Une Carte Postale de Paris

Chère Sophie,

Bonjour, c'est Jennifer, ta correspondante américaine. Je viens de passer une semaine à Paris, mais malheureusement tu étais en vacances. Je me suis vraiment amusée à Paris. Mes parents et moi avons visité le Louvre et le Musée d'Orsay où j'ai vu des peintures et des sculptures incroyables. Un soir nous sommes montés en haut de la Tour Eiffel à l'heure du crépuscule. Nous avons regardé le soleil se couche et l'ombre de la Tour sur les bâtiments en bas. Nous pouvions voir Sacré-Cœur, l'Arc de Triomphe, les Invalides, et les autres monuments. La nuit tous les monuments étaient illuminés et j'ai compris pourquoi Paris est nommé la Ville Lumière. Je dois t'avouer (confess) que j'ai adoré les crêpes qu'on vendait au coin de notre rue. J'ai pris de belles photos de notre aventure parisienne.

A bientôt, Jennifer

BRAIN TICKLERS
Set # 40

Read the following statements and mark them vrai or faux, true or false:

1. ____ The Romans were the first to settle Paris.

2. ____ The Louvre Palace was originally a fortress built to defend the city.

3. ____ The Tour Eiffel was built to be a permanent symbol of the city.

4. ____ Jennifer is a French girl.

5. ____ Jennifer and her family watched the sunset from the Eiffel Tower.

(Answers are on page 148.)

Joe Dassin *Les Champs-Elysées*
(Paroles et musique: Pierre Delanoé)

Je m'baladais sur l'avenue le cœur ouvert à l'inconnu
J'avais envie de dire bonjour à n'importe qui
N'importe qui et ce fut toi, je t'ai dit n'importe quoi
Il suffisait de te parler, pour t'apprivoiser

Aux Champs-Elysées, aux Champs-Elysées
Au soleil, sous la pluie, à midi ou à minuit
Il y a tout ce que vous voulez aux Champs-Elysées

Tu m'as dit "J'ai rendez-vous dans un sous-sol avec des fous
Qui vivent la guitare à la main, du soir au matin"
Alors je t'ai accompagnée, on a chanté, on a dansé
Et l'on n'a même pas pensé à s'embrasser

Aux Champs-Elysées, aux Champs-Elysées
Au soleil, sous la pluie, à midi ou à minuit
Il y a tout ce que vous voulez aux Champs-Elysées

Hier soir deux inconnus et ce matin sur l'avenue
Deux amoureux tout étourdis par la longue nuit
Et de l'Etoile à la Concorde, un orchestre à mille cordes
Tous les oiseaux du point du jour chantent l'amour

Aux Champs-Elysées, aux Champs-Elysées
Au soleil, sous la pluie, à midi ou à minuit
Il y a tout ce que vous voulez aux Champs-Elysées

Vocabulaire

se balader	to walk, stroll
l'inconnu	unknown
apprivoiser	to bring someone out of his or her shell
des fous	"crazies"
s'embrasser	to kiss
les amoureux	lovers
étourdis	dizzy, giddy

Amis/Faux Amis

A la mode, chic, and *élégant* are easy to recognize because they are also used in English; but did you notice several *faux amis* in the vocabulary?

> *Une chemise* is a shirt for men.
> *Un costume* is a suit, but it also refers to "costumes" in the theater.
> *Habits* means clothes in French.
> *Une robe* is a dress; you wear *une robe de chambre* over your pajamas.
> *Une veste* is a jacket or blazer; if you want a vest, you need *un gilet.*

BRAIN TICKLERS—THE ANSWERS

Set # 34, page 130

1. *Son pantalon est trop large.*
2. *Le pull est de taille moyenne.*
3. *Nous mettons des bottes en cuir.*
4. *Elle porte une robe bleue à pois.*
5. *Il préfère porter un jean bleu décoloré.*

Set # 35, page 133

1. *Nous nous couchons à dix heures et demie du soir.*
2. *Ils se lèvent à sept heures du matin.*
3. *Elle se maquille.*
4. *Ils se déshabillent maintenant.*
5. *Tu t'endors.*

Set # 36, page 135

A.
1. *quel . . . ce*
2. *quelles . . . ces*
3. *quelle . . . cette*
4. *quelles . . . ces*
5. *quel . . . cet*

B.
1. *Aimes-tu ce tee-shirt-ci ou ce tee-shirt-là?*
2. *Qui achète ce pull rouge?*
3. *Mon père aime cet anorak-ci en bleu, mais je préfère cet anorak-là en noir.*
4. *Est-ce que tu achètes ces chaussettes-ci en laine ou ces chaussettes-là en coton?*

Set # 37, page 137

A.
1. *plus*
2. *moins*
3. *aussi*
4. *plus*

B.
1. *La plus belle robe de soirée*
2. *Le chapeau le plus moche*
3. *Le meilleur maillot de bain*
4. *Le pyjama le plus drôle*
5. *Les plus vieilles chauss-ures*
6. *La veste la plus branchée*

Set # 38, page 140

A.
1. *Je m'habille en jean blanc.*
2. *Tu te maquilles avec du mascara.*
3. *Il se rase la figure.*
4. *Mes parents ne se couchent pas à neuf heures.*
5. *Vous allez vous promener au parc.*

B.
1. *rasoir*
2. *shampooing*
3. *cils*
4. *ongles*
5. *aisselles*
6. *boucles d'oreilles*

C.
Answers will vary.

Set # 39, page 142

A.
1. *Rends-moi mon sac à dos.*
2. *Rencontre-nous devant la boutique.*
3. *Passez-nous le dentifrice.*
4. *Apportez-moi ma veste du placard.*
5. *Prêtez-nous des gants.*

B.
1. *Levez-vous!*
2. *Asseyez-vous!*
3. *Promenez-vous au tableau!*
4. *Arrêtez-vous!*
5. *Coiffez-vous!*
6. *Asseyez-vous!*

Set # 40, page 145

1. *faux*
2. *vrai*
3. *faux*
4. *faux*
5. *vrai*

Vive les vacances: Faisons un voyage!

HURRAY FOR VACATION: LET'S TRAVEL!

Salut! C'est Sophie. Il est six heures du matin le premier août, et je me prépare à partir en vacances. Je me suis levée tôt ce matin pour mettre quelques derniers articles de toilette dans ma valise. Je me suis lavée et habillée, et je me suis brossé les dents. Maintenant nous partons à la mer à l'Ile de Ré sur la côte Atlantique. Nous voyageons en voiture avec toutes nos valises, Filou, notre chat, et Max, notre chien. Nous emportons toutes les choses dont nous aurons besoin pour passer le mois chez ma grand-mère qui habite une maison là-bas. Tous les ans nous aimons nous amuser à construire des châteaux de sable, nager, bronzer, et nous promener sur la plage. Cet été mon frère, Jean-Luc, va m'enseigner à faire de la planche à voile. C'est difficile, mais amusant. Le soir nous jouons aux cartes ou aux jeux de société avec toute la famille. Je ne m'ennuie jamais, mais mon amie Lucie me manque. Elle aussi, elle part en vacances avec sa famille à la montagne. Ils font du camping dans les Vosges dans l'est de la France. Ils vont rester dans un terrain de camping avec leur caravane. Quand elle peut, elle préfère dormir à la belle étoile dans son sac de couchage. Son père fait un feu et ils regardent les flammes en racontant des histoires pour passer les soirs. Pendant le jour ils font des randonnées dans la forêt, vont à la pêche, ou font du canoë dans un lac pittoresque. L'année dernière elle m'a envoyé une photo d'elle-même avec une grande truite (trout) qu'elle a attrapée. Nous nous écrivons des cartes postales, et je la reverrai en septembre.

Vocabulaire

Les Endroits	Places
un bois	woods, forest
un carnaval	carnival
une côte	coast, shore
un fleuve*	river
une forêt	forest
une île	island
une île tropicale	tropical island

un lac	lake
une mer	sea
un parc d'amusement	amusement park
un parc national	national park
une piste	trail
une piste de ski	ski trail
une plage	beach
une rive	bank (shore)
une rivière*	river
un ruisseau	stream
un terrain de camping	campground
un zoo	zoo

*To talk about a river that flows to a saltwater body, the French say *un fleuve*. A river that flows into *un fleuve* is *une rivière*. In France, the five *fleuves* are *la Garonne, la Loire, le Rhin, le Rhône,* and *la Seine*.

Proverbe: Didier dit

Les petits ruisseaux font les grandes rivières.
Great oaks from little acorns grow.
(Literally: Little streams become large rivers.)

La nature	Nature
l'abeille	bee
l'arbre	tree
l'arc-en-ciel	rainbow
le champ	field
le buisson	bush
le ciel	sky

l'étoile (f.)	star
la fleur	flower
la lune	moon
le moustique	mosquito
la plante	plant
le sable	sand
la terre	earth, dirt

Faire du camping	**Camping**
une allumette	match
une boussole	compass
une caravane	camper
un feu	fire
une poêle	frying pan
un sac à dos	backpack
un sac de couchage	sleeping bag
une tente	tent

Activités de vacances	**Vacation Activities**
aller à la chasse	to go hunting
aller à la pêche	to go fishing
se baigner	to have a swim
se bronzer	to get a tan
faire du bateau	to go boating
faire de la canoë	to go canoeing
faire de l'équitation	to go horseback riding
faire de la natation	to go swimming
faire du skate	to go skateboarding
faire de la planche à voiles	to go windsurfing
faire de la voile	to go sailing

faire du patin	to go skating
faire du roller	to go in-line skating
faire du ski	to go skiing
faire du ski nautique	to go waterskiing
faire du snow-boarding	to go snowboarding
faire une promenade	to go for a walk
faire un randonnée	to take a hike
Les moyens de transport	**Means of Transportation**
un autobus	bus
un autocar	tour bus
un avion	plane
un bateau	boat
un métro	subway
une mobylette	moped
une moto	motorcycle
un train	train
un tramway	tramway
un TGV*	high-speed train
un vélo	bike
une voiture	car

*TGV stands for *train à grande vitesse*. These French high-speed trains broke records in 2007 with a speed of 581 km per hour (361 mph). The TGV averages 254.5 km per hour or 158 mph, making travel between major cities in France extremely fast and comfortable. The track-laying techniques of French engineers are so remarkable that the train ride is extremely smooth.

Vocabulaire

Encore sur les transports	More on Transportation
un aéroport	airport
une agence de voyage	travel agency
un aller et retour	round-trip ticket
un aller simple	one-way ticket
un arrêt d'autobus	bus stop
une autoroute	highway
un billet	ticket
un chemin de fer	railroad
un composteur	machine to validate tickets
une gare	train station
un guichet	ticket window
une porte	gate
un quai	pier or platform
une rue	street

Info

> **Une vacance:** A vacancy, in a position to be filled, for example; it also means an "emptiness or void."
>
> **Les vacances:** We use the plural form in French to speak of vacations.
>
> **Vacances scolaires, universitaires:** School, university vacations.
>
> **Les grandes vacances:** The long summer vacation; in France this is traditionally at least four weeks for many workers and is taken in the summer months. The month of August is the traditional month on vacation for most workers in France, especially those who live and work in Paris.
>
> **Les petites vacances:** Those breaks of a few days or a week, such as the *vacances de Pâques,* or Easter vacation.

Fermeture annuelle: Annual closing for vacation of businesses, restaurants, theaters, and so on.

La rentrée: The "reentry" refers to the return to school and work after a vacation. In particular, *la rentrée* refers to September 1 when so many French people return from their August vacations, and school, business, and government offices resume normal schedules. This is like the week after Labor Day in the United States.

C'est curieux!

By law in France, essential businesses such as bakeries must coordinate their annual vacations: No town or neighborhood can be without a place to buy bread for a month!

Note these useful expressions:

aller en vacances: to go on vacation
prendre des/ses vacances: to take a/one's vacation
passer ses vacances: to spend one's vacation . . . à la montagne, au bord de la mer, à la campagne, à la neige, en France, à l'étranger, aux Etats-Unis

Encore c'est mieux
Expressions of Time

une journée	a day (long)
toute la journée	all day
quotidien/ne	daily
une semaine	a week
hebdomadaire	weekly
quinze jours	two weeks
tous les quinze jours	every two weeks
une quinzaine	about two weeks

Proverbe: Didier dit

Pierre qui roule n'amasse pas de mousse.
A rolling stone gathers no moss.

BRAIN TICKLERS
Set # 41

A. Give the French for the following words:

1. moon   4. stars

2. sky   5. sleeping bag

3. compass   6. tent

B. Write a short paragraph using the words from activity A.

C. Translate these sentences:

Conjugate *faire* (*je fais, tu fais, il/elle fait, nous faisons, vous faites, ils/elles font*)

1. We go fishing on the lake.

2. You (*tu*) go for a walk in the forest.

3. I go camping in the field.

4. My cousins go snowboarding on the ski trails.

5. Sophie goes windsurfing.

(Answers are on page 166.)

Proverbe: Didier dit

A qui se lève tôt, Dieu prête la main.
The early bird catches the worm.
(Literally: God helps early risers.)

Grammaire

Did you notice that Sophie said, *je me suis levée,* I got up early, and *je me suis habillée?* Reflexive verbs in the passé composé are conjugated with *être* as the helping verb. Notice the difference between the masculine and feminine spellings:

Se laver: to wash (yourself)

Masculine

Je me suis lavé	*Nous nous sommes lavés*
Tu t'es lavé	*Vous vous êtes lavé(s)*
Il s'est lavé	*Ils se sont lavés*

Feminine

Je me suis lavée	*Nous nous somme lavées*
Tu t'es lavée	*Vous vous êtes lavée(s)*
Elle s'est lavée	*Elles se sont lavées*

The reflexive pronoun can be either a **direct** or **indirect object pronoun**. In the preceding examples, the past participle *lavé* agrees with the subject pronoun because the reflexive pronouns act as direct object pronouns. They change to indirect object pronouns when there is a direct object pronoun after the verb.

> Monique s'est **lavé les mains**. Monique washed her hands.
> Mme François s'est **coupé les ongles**. Mrs. François cut her fingernails.
> Les enfants se sont **brossé les dents**. The children brushed their teeth.

Because *les mains, les ongles,* and *les dents* are the direct objects and come after the past participles, there is no agreement with the past participles (*lavé, coupé,* or *brossé*). This also occurs with reciprocal verbs that take **indirect object pronouns**:

se téléphoner à	to call each other
s'écrire	to write to each other
se parler	to talk to each other

> *Nous nous sommes parlé.* We talked to each other.
> (*nous* acts as an indirect object in this sentence)
> *Elles se sont écrit.* They wrote to each other.
> (*se* acts as an indirect object in this sentence)

BRAIN TICKLERS
Set # 42

Write these sentences in the past tense:

1. Les filles se réveillent tôt.

2. Nous nous parlons.

3. Pierre et Luc se brossent les cheveux.

4. Madeleine se prépare.

5. L'actrice se maquille les yeux.

(Answers are on page 166.)

Répète après moi!

The sound *-ille* is usually pronounced like a y as in yes: *une fille* (fiye), *elle se maquille* (mahkeeye), and *il se réveille* (rayvaye). There are a few exceptions: *mille* (meel), *ville* (veel), *tranquille* (trahnkeel); also *Lille* and *Deauville* have the pronounced l sound. Words that contain *-mille*, *-ville*, or *tranquille* also have the l sound.

Pronounce the following words with the l: *tranquillité, tranquilliser, millier* (about 1,000), *million, village, Deauville.*

These words have the y sound: *feuille, abeille, grenouille, maquillage, s'habiller, babiller* (to babble).

Encore c'est mieux

Comment parler des pays et des nationalité: How to Talk About
Countries and Nationalities

L'Allemagne	Germany	*allemand(e)*	German
L'Angleterre	England	*anglais(e)*	English
L'Australie	Australia	*australien(ne)*	Australian
La Belgique	Belgium	*belge*	Belgian
Le Canada	Canada	*canadien(ne)*	Canadian
La Chine	China	*chinois(e)*	Chinese
L'Ecosse	Scotland	*écossais(e)*	Scottish
L'Espagne	Spain	*espagnol(e)*	Spanish
Les Etats-Unis	United States	*américain(e)*	American
La France	France	*français(e)*	French
La Grèce	Greece	*grèc(que)*	Greek
L'Irlande	Ireland	*irlandais(e)*	Irish
l'Italie	Italy	*italien(ne)*	Italian
Le Japon	Japan	*japonais(e)*	Japanese
La Pologne	Poland	*polonais(e)*	Polish
Le Portugal	Portugal	*portugais(e)*	Portuguese
La Suisse	Switzerland	*suisse*	Swiss

RAPPEL!

Remember that nationalities are not generally
capitalized in French: ***Ils sont portugais**; je
suis américain. However, if you mean to say an American
or some Portuguese people, then capitalize: ***Un Américain a
acheté la villa**. An American bought the vacation home. **Des
Portugais l'ont louée**. Some Portuguese people rented it.

Grammaire
Prepositions with Geographical Expressions:

To express traveling *in* or *to* cities, countries, states, and
provinces, follow these guidelines:

à:	Cities	*à Paris*	to Paris
en: feminine	Countries	*en France*	to France
	Continents	*en Asie*	to Asia

	Provinces	*en Bretagne*	to Brittany
	States	*en Floride*	to Florida
au masculine*	Countries	*au Japon*	to Japan
		au Vietnam	to Vietnam
aux countries		*aux Pays Bas*	to the Netherlands
		aux Etats-Unis	to the United States

EXAMPLES:

*Ils voyagent **en** Chine pour visiter la Grande Muraille.*
They are traveling to China to visit the Great Wall.

*Nous allons passer quinze jours **au** Portugal.*
We are going to spend two weeks in Portugal.

*Je vais **au** Mexique.* I am going to Mexico.

*Les touristes voyagent **au** Cambodge.*
The tourists are traveling to Cambodia.

*The names of most countries are feminine and are easy to spot since they end in *e*. Most countries whose names end in any other letter are masculine. Two exceptions are *Le Mexique* (Mexico) and *Le Cambodge* (Cambodia).

Encore c'est mieux:

When talking about coming from places, use the following:

de (d'):	Cities	*de Montréal*	from Montreal
de (d'): Feminine	Countries	*de Belgique*	from Belgium
	Continents	*d'Australie*	from Australia
	Provinces	*de Normandie*	from Normandy
	States	*de Californie*	from California
du masculine	Countries	*du Sénégal*	from Senegal
		du Maroc	from Morocco
des plural	Countries	*des Etats-Unis*	from the United States

EXAMPLES:

*Mon oncle est **de** Suisse.*
My uncle is from Switzerland.

*Nous arrivons **de** Pennsylvanie.*
We are arriving from Pennsylvania.

*L'ambassadeur vient **du** Bénin.*
The ambassador comes from Benin.

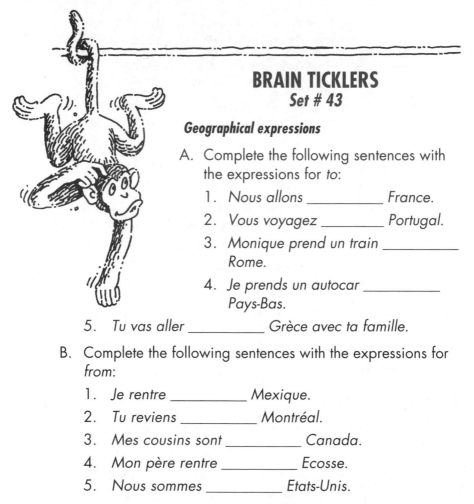

BRAIN TICKLERS
Set # 43

Geographical expressions

A. Complete the following sentences with the expressions for *to*:

1. *Nous allons _____ France.*
2. *Vous voyagez _____ Portugal.*
3. *Monique prend un train _____ Rome.*
4. *Je prends un autocar _____ Pays-Bas.*
5. *Tu vas aller _____ Grèce avec ta famille.*

B. Complete the following sentences with the expressions for *from*:

1. *Je rentre _____ Mexique.*
2. *Tu reviens _____ Montréal.*
3. *Mes cousins sont _____ Canada.*
4. *Mon père rentre _____ Ecosse.*
5. *Nous sommes _____ Etats-Unis.*

(Answers are on page 166.)

A réfléchir
Monaco

Monaco is a tiny country (less than 1 square mile [2.58 km²]) located along the Riviera or Mediterranean Sea just to the east of France. The total population is 39,646. Its history dates back to prehistoric peoples whose ancient relics dating from 200,000 years ago have been found in local caves. The Grimaldi family dominates the history of the principality of Monaco.

In 1297 François Grimaldi, disguised as a monk, entered the then walled city of Monaco and with his men (also in disguise) overthrew the town. The family has ruled Monaco since that time, surviving occupations by the Spanish and the French. The capital city, Monaco, sits on a large rock that juts out almost 3,000 feet into the sea and towers 200 feet above the shore. Visitors enjoy the Palace of the Prince, the Oceanographic Museum, and the picturesque side streets in this spotless town. There is an aquarium with water pumped directly from the sea into the lower part of the Oceanographic Museum. Tourists can see antique diving equipment as well as bones of giant squid and whales. In the lower part of Monaco is Monte Carlo, famous for its casino, Motor Rally, and Grand Prix. This race actually takes place on the winding streets of Monte Carlo at extremely high speeds. Of course the roads are closed off for this exciting event in May. The inhabitants of Monaco are exempt from paying taxes because of the financial success of the casino. The casino was established in 1878 and is surrounded by extensive gardens. Other industries, such as clothing, perfume, and pharmaceuticals, are being developed. The conference center also attracts international business conferences. Today Prince Albert II, the son of the late Prince Rainier and Princess Grace, formerly the American film actress Grace Kelly, continues to rule this small but dynamic country.

Tu sais quoi?

Albert I of Monaco was born in 1848 and became a sovereign at age twenty. He was an enthusiastic oceanographer. Albert invented a number of instruments and techniques used in exploration. Accompanied by renowned marine biologists, he went on numerous expeditions in his boat the Hirondelle II, which had a laboratory on board. He studied sea life and brought back specimens for his Oceanographic Institute, which he opened in 1910. He was also interested in the origins of humankind and was responsible for several archeological digs. The American Academy of Science awarded a gold medal to Prince Albert I in 1920 for his achievements.

Une Carte Postale de Monaco

Chère Sophie,

C'est Michel et je suis en voyage à Monaco. J'ai visité le Palais du Prince cet après-midi. Il y a une partie du Palais qui date du treizième siècle. On peut visiter le cours avec son magnifique escalier en marbre. On passe par la Halle d'Hercules où on peut voir des illustrations des histoires d'Hercules. Après on peut visiter plusieurs belles pièces décorées superbement. Il y a de vieux portraits et des miroirs impressionnants. Après la visite nous avons assisté au changement du garde qui s'appelle "le cérémonial de relève." Les gardes en beaux costumes s'appellent le Corps des Carabiniers, et ils font la relève tous les jours à 11h55. Après, nous avons déjeuné dans un petit café en face du palais. Nous n'avons pas vu le prince, mais il était en ville puisque le drapeau du Monaco flottait au-dessus du toit du palais. Sur le drapeau on voit deux moines qui représentent le début de l'histoire de la famille Grimaldi. Il fait beau mais un peu chaud; alors nous avons regardé la mer des Jardins de St. Martin. Je crois que c'est une des plus jolies vues que j'aie jamais vue. Plus tard nous allons visiter le Musée Océanographique.

A bientôt, Michel

Vocabulaire

treizième siècle	thirteenth century
la relève	changing of the guard
au-dessus	above
flotter	to float
un moine	monk
régner	to reign, rule

BRAIN TICKLERS
Set # 44

Determine if the following sentences are true (vrai) or false (faux) based on the Info and the Une Carte Postale sections. If the sentence is false, rewrite it to make it correct.

1. *La famille Grimaldi règne depuis 500,000 ans.*

2. *Le Palais du Prince n'est pas ouvert au public.*

3. *Dans le Musée Océanographique on peut voir des plantes exotiques.*

4. *En mai il y a une course d'automobile très célèbre: le Grand Prix.*

5. *Le prince François Grimaldi habite au Palais aujourd'hui.*

(Answers are on page 166.)

Amis/Faux Amis

Among the vocabulary in this chapter, you may have recognized the following *amis*: *aéroport, zoo, lac, île, arbre* (arbor, tree). But be careful of the following *faux amis*:

Rive means bank or shore, not river.
Un autocar, or *car*, is a touring bus.
Circulation means traffic.

BRAIN TICKLERS — THE ANSWERS

Set # 41, page 157

A.
1. *la lune*
2. *le ciel*
3. *la boussole*
4. *les étoiles*
5. *le sac de couchage*
6. *la tente*

B.
Answers will vary.

C.
1. *Nous faisons de la pêche sur le lac.*
2. *Tu fais une promenade dans la forêt.*
3. *Je fais du camping dans le champ.*
4. *Mes cousins font du snow-boarding sur les pistes de ski.*
5. *Sophie fait de la planche à voile.*

Set # 42, page 159

1. *Les filles se sont réveillées tôt.*
2. *Nous nous sommes parlé.*
3. *Pierre et Luc se sont brossé les cheveux.*
4. *Madeleine s'est préparée.*
5. *L'actrice s'est maquillé les yeux.*

Set # 43, page 162

A.
1. *en*
2. *au*
3. *à*
4. *aux*
5. *en*

B.
1. *du*
2. *de*
3. *du*
4. *d'*
5. *des*

Set # 44, page 165

1. *faux. La famille Grimaldi règne depuis plus de 7 siècles.*
2. *faux. Le palais du Prince est ouvert au public.*
3. *faux. Dans le Musée Océanographique on peut voir des poissons exotiques.*
4. *vrai*
5. *faux. Le prince Albert II habite au Palais aujourd'hui.*

Ce que je voudrais faire plus tard: Occupations

WHAT I WANT TO DO LATER IN LIFE: OCCUPATIONS

Salut! C'est Sophie. Ça va? Qu'est-ce que tu veux faire plus tard? Moi, je veux faire de la médicine. Je voudrais aider les autres, et je trouve les sciences fascinantes. Il faut alors réussir à mes études pour pouvoir aller à une université de médecin. Je finirai mon bac en cinq ans et je devrai étudier pour encore longtemps avant de devenir médecin. Si j'ai l'occasion de voyager j'aimerai voir le monde un peu. Je considérerai travailler avec les Médecins Sans Frontières pour gagner de l'expérience et pour aider les pauvres. Plus tard s'il est possible je vivrai à Paris. Mon frère, Jean-Luc, sera diplômé en juin et il étudiera le droit pour être avocat. Lui aussi, il devra étudier assez longtemps. Il est très intelligent et je sais qu'il réussira. Mon père est avocat et ma mère est musicienne. Ils soutiennent que nous pouvons faire ce que nous voulons faire avec du travail. Lucie voudrait, elle aussi, faire de la médicine, mais elle préfère travailler avec les animaux. Avec de la chance elle sera vétérinaire, autrement elle fera peut-être des recherches sur les animaux. Son père est professeur de sciences et sa mère est écrivain. Ils l'encouragent à explorer plusieurs choix de professions.

Info

Médecins Sans Frontières (MSF), Doctors Without Borders, is an international humanitarian aid organization founded in 1971 that provides emergency medical assistance to populations in danger in more than seventy countries. It is a private nonprofit association that has no political, economic, or religious connections. It has a large-scale ability to provide specialized medical kits quickly to people in need. To learn more about them, visit *www.doctorswithoutborders.org.*

Vocabulaire	
Les professions	**Professions**
un acteur (une actrice)	actor
un/e architecte	architect
un/une artiste	artist

un/une avocat(e)	lawyer
un/une boucher(ère)	butcher
un/une boulanger(ère)	baker
un charpentier	carpenter
un chef	chef
un compositeur	composer
un/une cuisinier(ière)	cook
un/une dentiste	dentist
un écrivain	writer
un/une électricien(ne)	electrician
un facteur (une factrice)	mail carrier
une fille/un jeune homme au pair	an au pair
un gérant(e)	manager
un/une infirmier(ière)	nurse
un ingénieur	engineer
un instituteur(trice)	teacher (primary school)
un juge	judge
un médecin	doctor
un metteur en scène	director (in theater)
un/une musicien(ne)	musician
un peintre	painter
un/une pharmacien(ne)	pharmacist
un/une photographe	photographer
un plombier(ière)	plumber
un pompier	firefighter
un professeur	teacher
un/une prof	professor, teacher (secondary)

un/une programmeur(euse)	programmer
un réalisateur(trice)	director (movie, TV)
un/une responsable	head, person in charge
un savant	scientist/scholar
un/une sécrétaire	secretary
un/une serveur(euse)	waiter/ waitress
un superviseur	manager, overseer
un/une traducteur(trice)	translator
un/une vendeur(euse)	salesperson
un vétérinaire	veterinarian

C'est curieux!

Most nouns designating a profession have a masculine and a feminine form. Some, however, remain in the masculine and may refer to a man or a woman. Gradually, the French language is accepting feminine forms for professions once considered for men only: *une juge, une proviseure* (head of school).

But do not confuse *médecin* and *médecine*. *Un médecin* is a doctor, and we use this form for masculine or feminine subjects. *La médecine* refers to the practice or study of medicine.

Vocabulaire

Endroits de travail	Workplaces
une banque	bank
un bâtiment	building
un bureau	office
un bureau de poste	post office
un centre commercial	mall, shopping center, office park
un édifice	building
un gratte-ciel	skyscraper

un hôpital	hospital
une librairie	bookstore
une mairie	town hall
un palais de justice	courthouse
une pharmacie	drugstore
un poste d'incendie	firehouse
une station-service	gas station
un théâtre	theater
une usine	factory
Des expressions du temps futur	**Future Time Expressions**
à l'avenir	in the future
l'année prochaine	next year
aussitôt que	as soon as
bientôt	soon
demain	tomorrow
dès que	as soon as
en dix ans	in ten years
l'été prochain	next summer
lorsque	when, at the time
plus tard	later
quand	when
un jour	someday

ATTENTION!

When speaking of professions with the verbs *être* and *devenir*, do not use articles: *Mon père **est avocat***. My father is a lawyer. *Ma mère **est musicienne***. My mother is a musician. *Mon frère **devient aussi avocat***. My brother is also becoming a lawyer.

But when the profession is modified, articles are used: *C'est **un bon médecin***. He's a good doctor. *C'est **une jolie actrice***. She's a pretty actress.

Proverbe: Didier dit

C'est en forgeant qu'on devient forgeron.
Practice makes perfect.
(Literally: It's by forging that you become a blacksmith.)

BRAIN TICKLERS
Set # 45

A. Name where the following professionals would work.

Ex: *le professeur: le collège, le lycée*

1. *l'infirmier*
2. *le juge*
3. *le facteur*
4. *un secrétaire*
5. *un plombier*
6. *un acteur*

B. Translate these future espressions:

1. soon
2. someday
3. when (at the time)
4. later
5. next summer

(Answers are on page 189.)

Info

The French novelist Jules Verne (1828–1905), who was fascinated by the great progress in science and the inventions of the nineteenth century, is considered along with H. G. Wells to be the originator of what we call science fiction. Verne did not have a scientific or technical background, but he did a great deal of research in writing his books so the details would appear practical and realistic. It is his sense of adventure and imagination about the future that make his work so popular even today. He was one of the first, for example, to imagine human flight to the moon, and in *Twenty Thousand Leagues Under the Sea* (1869–1870), he created an elaborate submarine for the character of Captain Nemo. That submarine, the *Nautilus*, is one of many examples from Verne's fiction to become fact later. Verne's novels are often in the form of amazing journeys, including

Journey to the Center of the Earth (1864) and *Around the World in 80 Days* (1873). Several of Verne's novels have also been made into successful movies in both Europe and the United States.

Grammaire
Le temps futur (The Future Tense)

In English we say that we "will do something" and add the word **will** to the verb. In French the future is expressed with a single verb form: *je **voyagerai** l'été prochain.* I **will** travel next summer. *Nous **travaillerons** en ville.* We **will work** in town.

For *-er* and *-ir* verbs, the future is formed by adding the future endings to the infinitive:

Parler (to speak)

Je parlerai	I will speak
Tu parleras	You will speak

Il/Elle parlera	He/She will speak
Nous parlerons	We will speak
Vous parlerez	You will speak
Ils/Elles parleront	They will speak

Finir (to finish)

Je finirai	*Nous finirons*
Tu finiras	*Vous finirez*
Il/Elle finira	*Ils/Elles finiront*

With *-re* verbs and many irregular verbs that end in *-re,* drop the e:

Vendre (to sell)

Je vendrai	*Nous vendrons*
Tu vendras	*Vous vendrez*
Il/Elle vendra	*Ils/Elles vendront*

Boire (to drink)

Je boirai	*Nous boirons*
Tu boiras	*Vous boirez*
Il/Elle boira	*Ils/Elles boiront*

Conduire: je conduirai	I will drive
Connaître: je connaîtrai	I will know (be acquainted)
Croire: je croirai	I will believe
Dire: je dirai	I will say
Ecrire: j'écrirai	I will write
Lire: je lirai	I will read
Mettre: je mettrai	I will put on
Reconnaître: je reconnaîtrai	I will recognize
Traduire: je traduirai	I will translate

BRAIN TICKLERS
Set # 46

A. Rewrite the verbs in these sentences about *le quatorze juillet* in the future tense:

1. Tu *écoutes* le maire.

2. Nous *regardons* les feux d'artifices. (fireworks)

3. Pierre *vend* des petits drapeaux français.

4. Mon père *conduit* au parc.

5. Mes cousines *mettent* des tee-shirts rouges.

B. Translate these sentences into English:

1. *Tu me donneras l'adresse de ton correspondant.*

2. *Je téléphonerai à son appartement à Paris.*

3. *Il nous invitera à faire un pique-nique.*

4. *Toute la famille mangera au parc.*

5. *Je t'écrirai un mail.*

6. *Je m'amuserai!*

C. Translate these sentences into French:

1. I will finish soon.

2. We will arrive by train.

3. She will telephone you later.

4. Who will answer this letter?

5. When will they write?

(Answers are on page 189.)

Répète après moi!

When you speak in the future tense, the a ending is strong and clearly pronounced like ah. When you see words you know in English, it is tempting to pronounce them in English. Concentrate on keeping the a sound open—as if you were at the dentist—ah and ahn when followed by n or m. Carefully say these words with a French accent:

Future tense: *Il jouera, tu danseras, elle rentrera, il sera, il aura* (future tense), (He will play, you will dance, she will return, he will be, he will have); *Canada, facteur, lac, arbre, café, palais, girafe, gratte-ciel, savant, éléphant, plante,* (Canada, mail carrier, lake, tree, coffee, palace, giraffe, skyscraper, scientist, elephant, plant.)

Grammaire
Le temps futur des verbes irréguliers
(The Future Tense of Irregular Verbs)

A number of verbs have irregular stems in the future tense. They use the same endings as regular verbs. Memorize their forms:

avoir: to have

J'aurai	I will have	*Nous aurons*	We will have
Tu auras	You will have	*Vous aurez*	You will have
Il/Elle aura	He/She will have	*Ils/Elles auront*	They will have

First Person (je) and Third Person (il) Singular Forms of Some Irregular Verbs:

Aller	to go	*j'irai*	I will go
Courir	to run	*je courrai*	I will run
Devoir	to have to	*je devra*	I have to
Envoyer	to send	*j'enverrai*	I will send
Etre	to be	*je serai*	I will be
Faire	to do/make	*je ferai*	I will do
Falloir	to be necessary	*il faudra*	It will be necessary
Mourir	to die	*je mourrai*	I will die
Pleuvoir	to rain	*il pleuvra*	It will rain
Pouvoir	to be able	*je pourrai*	I will be able
Recevoir	to receive	*je recevrai*	I will receive
Savoir	to know	*je saurai*	I will know
Voir	to see	*je verrai*	I will see
Vouloir	to want	*je voudrai*	I will want

Proverbe: Didier dit

Rira bien qui rira le dernier.
He who laughs last laughs best.

ATTENTION!

When you talk about the future in French, do not use the present tense with "when."

*Quand **j'aurai** vingt ans j'irai à Paris.* When I am (will be) twenty years old, I will go to Paris.

*Lorsque tu le **verras**, tu le reconnaîtras.* When you see him, you will recognize him.

Vocabulaire

Encore c'est mieux

____ € par heure	$____per hour
une augmentation de salaire	a raise
avoir une maîtrise	to have a master's degree
un client	customer
un/une employé(e)	employee
être diplômé	to have a degree
être en chômage	to be unemployed
être en retraite	to be retired
étudiant	college or university student
embaucher	to hire
la formation	training
en grève	on strike
disponible	available
un jour de congé	a day off
un/une patron(ne)	boss
renvoyer	to fire
un salaire	a salary
un stage	internship
travailler à mi-temps	work part time

Vive la différence!

Students in French schools rarely have after-school jobs. They help out with household chores, but they are not expected to work after school. Unlike American teens, they rarely save up for a car or other large purchases while in school. Their school day lasts until 4 or 5 o'clock and they usually have two or three hours of homework each night.

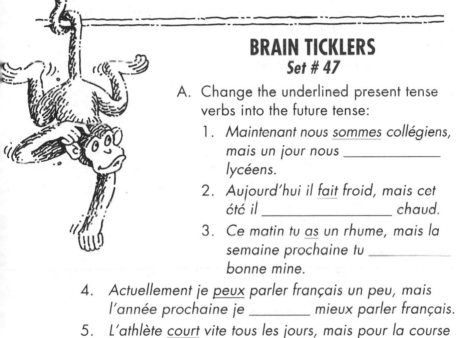

BRAIN TICKLERS
Set # 47

A. Change the underlined present tense verbs into the future tense:

1. *Maintenant nous __sommes__ collégiens, mais un jour nous _____ lycéens.*

2. *Aujourd'hui il __fait__ froid, mais cet été il _____ chaud.*

3. *Ce matin tu __as__ un rhume, mais la semaine prochaine tu _____ bonne mine.*

4. *Actuellement je __peux__ parler français un peu, mais l'année prochaine je _____ mieux parler français.*

5. *L'athlète __court__ vite tous les jours, mais pour la course (race) il _____ plus vite.*

6. *Maintenant l'enfant __va__ à l'école maternelle, mais l'année prochaine il _____ à l'école primaire.*

B. Translate these sentences:

1. The lawyer will be retired in ten years.

2. I will have a diploma in five years.

3. We will want to work at the hospital.

4. Marie will have her master's degree in one year.

5. Next month the employees will receive a day off.

(Answers are on page 189.)

Info

The French are of course very interested in the future, and they even have a theme park to explore, called **Futuroscope**. It was built in 1987 not far from the central city of Poitiers. It is the only theme park of its kind in Europe. The buildings are built of futuristic materials in spheres, pyramids, and other intriguing shapes surrounded by pristine gardens. Spectacular science expositions that change regularly can be viewed on a variety of screens from Hemispheric, a room with 850 television screens in an expansive 900 square meters. The park caters to science fiction fans and thrill seekers alike with a variety of exciting rides and thought-provoking films and interactive exhibits. Check it out on its website, *en.futuroscope.com*.

Grammaire
Le temps conditionnel (The Conditional Tense)

Now that you've studied the future tense, you will learn the conditional tense: "I would like," *je voudrais*, was introduced in a previous chapter. When we form the conditional tense in English, we add the word "would" to the verb. In French it is a single verb form. Adding the endings for the imperfect tense to the future tense stem forms it.

It is generally used under a condition or hypothetical situation, as in these examples:

> *Si j'étais français,* If I <u>were</u> French,
>
> *Je <u>mangerais</u> un croissant tous les jours!* I <u>would eat</u> a croissant every day!
>
> *Tu <u>serais</u> heureux de visiter le Côte d'Azur.* You <u>would be</u> happy to visit the Riviera.
>
> *Pierre <u>participerait</u> au Tour de France.* Pierre <u>would participate</u> in the Tour de France.
>
> *Françoise <u>travaillerait</u> dans une pâtisserie.* Françoise <u>would work</u> in a pastry shop.
>
> *Nous <u>conduirions</u> des mobylettes.* We <u>would drive</u> mopeds.
>
> *Vous ne <u>résisteriez</u> pas les escargots.* You <u>wouldn't resist</u> the snails.

Mes amis iraient en colonie de vacances. My friends would go to summer camp.

Les filles choisiraient du parfum français. The girls would choose French perfume.

Note that the preceding verbs use the **future stem** plus **imperfect endings**.

Rappel: Using the *nous* form stem of a verb and the following endings forms the imperfect tense. Notice that in general the conditional tense is longer than the imperfect and always has an « *r* » before the ending. Compare these imperfect verbs to their conditional forms:

L'imparfait		*Le conditionnel*	
Je mangeais	I was eating	*je mangerais*	I would eat
Tu étais	You were	*tu serais*	You would be
Il participait	He used to participate	*il participerait*	He would participate
Elle travaillait	She was working	*elle travaillerait*	She would work
Nous conduisions	We were driving	*nous conduirions*	We would drive
Vous ne résistiez pas	You were not resisting	*vous ne résisteriez pas*	You would not resist
Ils allaient	They used to go	*ils iraient*	They would go
Elles choisissaient	They were choosing	*elles choisiraient*	They would choose

Grammaire
Les Clauses Si (If Clauses)

"If" clauses (*Si j'étais français je parlerais français tout le temps*, If I were French I would speak French all the time) follow strict patterns. There are several patterns:

1. *Si* clause in the present; resultant clause in the present, future, or imperative
2. *Si* clause in the imperfect; resultant clause in the conditional

   Si tu **veux** *partir, tu* **peux**. If you **want** to leave, you **can**.
   present   **present**

*Si tu **veux** partir, tu **voyageras** cet été.* If you **want** to leave, you **will travel** this summer.
    present   **future**

*Si tu **veux** partir, **téléphone**-moi.* If you **want** to leave, **telephone** me.
    present   **imperative (command)**

*Si tu **voulais** partir, tu **pourrais**.* If you **wanted** to leave, you **could**.
    imperfect   **conditional**

The "if" clause part of the sentence may occur in the second part of the sentence, but the other verb must fit the preceding pattern.

*Il me **téléphone** s'il **visite** les Etats-Unis.*	He calls me if he visits the United States.
*Nous **regarderons** la télé s'il **pleut**.*	We will watch TV if it rains.
*Tu **courrais** vite **si** tu **voyais** un ours!*	You would run fast if you saw a bear.

ATTENTION!

Si means "if" and becomes *s'* in front of *il* but not in front of *elle*:

*Répondez **s'il** vous plaît.* Answer if you please. (RSVP)
(an "if" clause you already know!)
*Elle répondra **si elle** peut venir.*
    She will answer if she can come.

BRAIN TICKLERS
Set # 48

A. Use the imperfect or the conditional tense to complete the "if" clause. Identify the tense of the verb provided to know which tense to write:

Ex: *Tu serais (conditionnel) contente si tu __étais__ (imparfait) au parc. (être)*

1. *Si j'_____ deux cents dollars je m'achèterais* une tablette. (avoir)*

2. *Si tu avais le temps tu _____ un voyage en Chine. (faire)*

3. *Nous resterions deux mois si nous _____. (pouvoir)*

4. *Vous ririez si vous _____ son histoire. (entendre)*

5. *Si Thomas _____ à son examen, ses parents seraient heureux. (réussir)*

B. Now use the present, future, or imperative command to complete these sentences:

1. *Si tu aimes les animaux tu _____ vétérinaire.* (will become)

2. *Si nous travaillons bien nous _____ tôt.* (finish)

3. *Attends-moi si tu _____ en avance.* (arrive)

4. *_____ la radio si tu veux savoir les nouvelles.* (Listen to)

5. *L'ingénieur _____ une augmentation de salaire s'il gagne un prix.* (will receive)

(Answers are on page 189.)

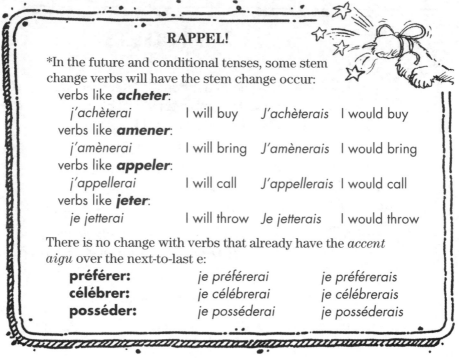

RAPPEL!

*In the future and conditional tenses, some stem change verbs will have the stem change occur:

verbs like **acheter**:

| j'achèterai | I will buy | J'achèterais | I would buy |

verbs like **amener**:

| j'amènerai | I will bring | J'amènerais | I would bring |

verbs like **appeler**:

| j'appellerai | I will call | J'appellerais | I would call |

verbs like **jeter**:

| je jetterai | I will throw | Je jetterais | I would throw |

There is no change with verbs that already have the *accent aigu* over the next-to-last e:

préférer:	je préférerai	je préférerais
célébrer:	je célébrerai	je célébrerais
posséder:	je posséderai	je posséderais

Info
Victor Hugo

Born in Besançon, France, in 1802, Victor Hugo had an interesting childhood during which he accompanied his father, one of Bonaparte's generals, on campaigns to Italy and Spain. He spent some time studying in Madrid before returning to Paris to live with his mother. He studied math and poetry in school. At age twenty he gave up math to concentrate on literature when he published *Odes*. He married Adèle Foucher in that same year. Hugo wrote the novels *Hunchback of Notre Dame*, called *Notre Dame de Paris* in French, and *Les Misérables*. He wrote poetry, plays, and novels during his long lifetime. He entered politics and had to live in exile during a period of his life. He had four children whom he adored. When his daughter Léopoldine died tragically in a boating accident during her honeymoon, he was devastated. It is said that her new husband died trying to save her. On the fourth anniversary of her death, Victor Hugo wrote the following poem. He lived to the age of eighty-three and upon his death had one of the largest Parisian funerals of all times.

Demain, dès l'aube . . .

Demain, dès l'aube, à l'heure où blanchit la campagne,
Je partirai. Vois-tu, je sais que tu m'attends.
J'irai par la forêt, j'irai par la montagne.
Je ne puis demeurer loin de toi plus longtemps.

Je marcherai les yeux fixés sur mes pensées,
Sans rien voir au dehors, sans entendre aucun bruit,
Seul, inconnu, le dos courbé, les mains croisées,
Triste, et le jour pour moi sera comme la nuit.

Je ne regarderai ni l'or du soir qui tombe,
Ni les voiles au loin descendant vers Harfleur,
Et quand j'arriverai, je mettrai sur la tombe
Un bouquet de houx vert et de bruyère en fleur.

Vocabulaire

l'aube	sunrise
blanchit	whitens
Je ne puis . . . plus	I can no longer
fixés	fixed
au dehors	outside
aucun	not a single
bruit	sound
courbé	curved
croisées	crossed
l'or	gold
les voiles	sails
houx	holly
bruyère	heather

A réfléchir: The Maghreb

The Maghreb is the name of the northern region of Africa. Maghreb means "place of the sunset" or "western" in Arabic. It is north of the Sahara Desert and west of the Nile. The French-speaking countries of this region are Algeria, Morocco, and Tunisia. All three countries were French colonies until the mid-1950s. The people are a mixture of Berber and Arabs with a small percentage of Europeans. In Algeria the European minority were called *pied-noirs*; however, most left Algeria after the French colonial period ended. The religion is primarily Muslim (99 percent), although there are small Christian and Jewish populations. A dish typical of this region is couscous. It is a small round grain served with vegetables and/or meat like lamb, chicken, or beef. It can be mild or *très piquant* (very spicy). The Kasbah is an architectural tradition with old towns with narrow streets and whitewashed walls. Towns in Morocco are often named after *marabouts*, or saints. Casablanca is probably the most famous and largest city of Morocco, although the capital is Rabat. Its man-made port is the largest in North Africa. It is also home to the second largest mosque (over 100,000 worshippers can be accommodated) in the world, the Hassan II Mosque. It has a tower or minaret that is 210 meters tall and it is located on a hill looking over the Atlantic. An interesting fact is that Morocco was the first foreign country to establish diplomatic relations with the United States (in 1787), and its Treaty of Peace and Friendship is the longest unbroken treaty relationship in U.S. history.

Une Carte Postale de Maroc

Chère Sophie,

Comment ça va? C'est Raoul, et je t'écris de Casablanca au Maroc. C'est ici où j'habite avec ma famille. J'ai de la chance d'assister à l'école américaine ici. Nous apprenons à parler français, anglais, et arabe (ma langue natale). Nous avons des cours en chaque langue selon le niveau de classe. Je fais des maths en anglais mais l'histoire en arabe. Nous participons dans beaucoup de voyages scolaires pour pratiquer les langues et étudier notre environnement. Nous avons fait un tour dans le Sahara à chameau. C'était amusant! Nous avons traversé des dunes pour arriver à des oasis. La chaleur était accablante, mais nous avons porté des robes spéciales pour nous protéger du soleil et du sable. Je t'invite à venir me rendre visite. Nous pouvons aller au marché Derb Gallef. Je voudrais te montrer ma ville moderne mais encore historique.

Ecris-moi, Raoul

Vocabulaire

un chameau	camel
la chaleur	heat
accablante	overwhelming

BRAIN TICKLERS
Set # 49

Vrai ou faux: Mark whether the following sentences are true or false. Then correct the false statements.

1. Tunisia, Morocco, and Algeria form the Sahara Desert.

2. The capital of Morocco is Casablanca.

3. The United States and Morocco do not have a diplomatic relationship.

4. The largest port in North Africa is in Tunisia.

5. English, French, and Arabic are taught in school.

(Answers are on page 190.)

Amis/Faux Amis

Among the names of professions, there are many good *amis*: *architect*, *artiste*, *juge*, and so on. But remember not to confuse these *faux amis*:

> *Une librairie* is a bookstore; the library is a *bibliothèque*.
> *Une bibliothéquaire* or *une documentaliste* is a librarian.
> *Un médecin* is a doctor; *la médecine* refers to medicine.

BRAIN TICKLERS—THE ANSWERS

Set # 45, page 173

A.
1. *l'hôpital*
2. *le palais de justice*
3. *la poste*
4. *le bureau*
5. *la maison*
6. *le théâtre*

B.
1. *bientôt*
2. *un jour*
3. *lorsque*
4. *plus tard*
5. *l'été prochain*

Set # 46, page 175

A.
1. *Tu écouteras*
2. *Nous regarderons*
3. *Pierre vendra*
4. *Mon père conduira*
5. *Mes cousines mettront*

B.
1. You will give me your pen pal's address.
2. I will call his apartment in Paris.
3. He will invite us to go on a picnic.
4. The whole family will eat at the park.
5. I will write you an email.
6. I will have a good time!

C.
1. *Je finirai bientôt.*
2. *Nous arriverons en train.*
3. *Elle te (vous) téléphonera plus tard.*
4. *Qui répondra à cette lettre?*
5. *Quand est-ce qu'ils écriront?*

Set # 47, page 179

A.
1. *serons*
2. *fera*
3. *auras*
4. *pourrai*
5. *courra*
6. *ira*

B.
1. *L'avocat sera en retraite en dix ans.*
2. *J'aurai mon diplôme en cinq ans.*
3. *Nous voudrons travailler à l'hôpital.*
4. *Marie aura sa maîtrise en un an.*
5. *Le mois prochain les employés recevront un jour de congé.*

Set # 48, page 183

A.
1. *avais* (imp.)
2. *ferais* (cond.)
3. *pouvions* (imp.)
4. *entendiez* (imp.)
5. *réussissait* (imp.)

B.
1. *deviendras*
2. *finissons*
3. *arrives*
4. *Ecoute*
5. *recevra*

Set # 49, page 187

1. *faux; The Maghreb*
2. *faux; Rabat*
3. *faux; the Treaty of Peace and Friendship*
4. *faux; Rabat, Morocco*
5. *vrai*

J'aime la terre: L'environnement

I CARE ABOUT THE EARTH: THE ENVIRONMENT

Salut! C'est Sophie. J'adore la nature. S'il fait beau il faut que je sorte explorer. Si je suis en ville je cherche des nouvelles fleurs comme des myosotis (forget-me-nots) au parc où je peux aussi voir des petits moineaux ou des pigeons paresseux qui cherchent quelque chose à manger. J'aime voir les papillons et les abeilles qui fréquentent les fleurs épanouies. Le dimanche nous faisons des piques-niques à la campagne. J'aime m'asseoir sous un vieux chêne pour regarder les écureuils dans les branches de l'arbre. Je les trouve adorables.

Ma mère connaît les chants d'oiseaux et elle peut identifier le chant d'un cardinal ou d'un geai. Elle est contente que je sois une bonne élève et que j'apprenne vite à les reconnaître aussi. Je me sens triste qu'il y ait parfois des détritus par terre. Les vieux papiers ou les bouteilles en plastique qu'on jette me font horreur. Comment peut-on jeter des choses par terre? Il faut que nous nous occupions de notre environnement. Nous faisons du recyclage à la maison, ça veut dire que nous séparons les journaux et le verre pour mettre dans les réceptacles de recyclage. Et toi, fais-tu du recyclage chez toi?

Vocabulaire

Oiseaux	Birds
un aigle	eagle
une alouette	lark
un faucon	falcon
un cardinal	cardinal
une chouette	owl
un colibri	hummingbird
une colombe	dove
un geai bleu	blue jay
un moineau	sparrow

Animaux de la forêt	Forest Animals
un castor	beaver
un cerf	deer
un écureuil	squirrel
une grenouille	frog
une marmotte	groundhog
une mouffette	skunk
un ours	bear
un porc-épic	porcupine
un sanglier	boar
un serpent	snake

Insectes	Insects
une abeille	bee
une araignée	spider
une chenille	caterpillar
une coccinelle	ladybug
une mouche	fly
un moustique	mosquito
un papillon	butterfly

Mots miscellanées	Miscellaneous Words
des détritus	litter
des fleurs épanouies	flowers in bloom
un chêne	oak
le recyclage	recycling
la pollution	pollution

Endroits dans la nature	Places in Nature
un champ	field
une chute d'eau	waterfall
une colline	hill
un désert	desert

un étang	pond
une grotte	cave
une île	island
un lac	lake
une montagne	mountain
une plage	beach
une prairie	prairie
un ruisseau	stream
le sable	sand
une source	spring
une vallée	valley

BRAIN TICKLERS
Set # 50

A. Translate these words:

1. skunk
2. spring
3. island
4. ladybug
5. falcon
6. hill
7. sparrow
8. lark
9. butterfly
10. oak

B. Now write five sentences using other nature vocabulary words.

C. Ask your teacher to teach you how to sing *Alouette*.

Alouette, gentille alouette,
  Alouette, je te plumerai.

  Je te plumerai la tête {×2}
  Et la tête {×2}
  Alouette {×2}
  Ah!

Je te plumerai le bec {×2}
Et le bec {×2}
Et la tête {×2}
Alouette {×2}
Ah!

Je te plumerai les yeux
Je te plumerai le cou
Je te plumerai les ailes
Je te plumerai les pattes
Je te plumerai la queue
Je te plumerai le dos

(Answers are on page 212.)

Proverbe: Didier dit

Petit à petit l'oiseau fait son nid. Rome wasn't built in a day.
(Literally: Little by little the bird builds its nest.)

Grammaire
L'imperatif (Commands)

In previous chapters you have seen some commands used with
-er verbs and with object pronouns. Commands are used only in
addressing someone directly. The subject is understood because
you are addressing the individual. You therefore find only three
forms of commands: *tu*, you informal; *vous*, you formal or polite;
and *nous*, let's. With most verbs simply use those conjugated
verb forms without the subject pronoun.

Your teacher might say:
　　Finis ta rédaction! Finish your composition!
　　　　(speaking to one student)
　　Finissez les devoirs! Finish the homework!
　　　　(speaking to all the students)

The students might suggest:
　　Finissons le film! Let's finish the movie!

With *-er* verbs you may remember that the s is dropped from the *tu* form:

Regarde l'écureuil! Look at the squirrel!
Ecoute l'oiseau! Listen to the bird!

The *vous* and *nous* forms have no changes:

Regardez les papillons! Look at the butterflies!
Ecoutons la chouette! Let's listen to the owl!

There are three exceptions: ***être***, ***avoir***, and ***savoir***. Study their forms:

	Sois	be
Etre:	*Soyez*	be
To be	*Soyons*	let's be
	Aie	have
Avoir:	*Ayez*	have
To have	*Ayons*	let's have
	Sache	know
Savoir:	*Sachez*	know
To know	*Sachons*	let's know

To make commands negative, simply sandwich the verb with the negative expression:

Ne sois pas paresseux! Don't be lazy!
N'ayez pas peur! Don't be afraid!
N'écoutons pas ce CD. Let's not listen to this CD.
Ne traverse jamais la rue sans regarder. Never cross the road without looking.
Ne chantez plus! Don't sing anymore!

BRAIN TICKLERS
Set # 51

A. Use the imperative to form commands with the verbs indicated:

1. _____ l'abeille. (Ne pas toucher) (tu)

2. _____ les cerfs. (photographier) (vous)

3. _____ à manger aux pigeons. (ne pas donner) (vous)

4. _____ du recyclage. (faire) (nous)

5. _____ les fleurs épanouies. (ne pas couper) (tu)

B. Unscramble these vocabulary words and translate them.

1. _____phcam_____

2. _____roeusc_____

3. _____licenleh_____

4. _____agie eulb_____

5. _____fouttemef_____

(Answers are on page 212.)

Proverbe: Didier dit

Il n'y a pas de rose sans épine.
There is no rose without thorns.

Vocabulaire: Encore c'est mieux

arroser	to water
cueillir	to pick
défricher	to cultivate
enlever les mauvaises herbes	to weed
fleurir	to bloom, to flower
planter	to plant
tailler	to prune
tondre le gazon	to mow the lawn

Des fleurs et des plantes — Flowers and Plants

un buisson	bush
un chrysanthème	chrysanthemum
un dahlia	dahlia
une fougère	fern
l'herbe	grass
un iris	iris
une jonquille	daffodil
un lys	lily
une marguerite	daisy
une mauvaise herbe	weed
un muguet	lily of the valley
un myosotis	forget-me-not
un pétunia	petunia
une rose	rose
un tournesol	sunflower

Vive la différence!

Flowers have special meaning in France. On May 1, May Day, vendors sell sprigs of lily of the valley, *muguet*, to people who buy them to offer to friends. Roses represent love, especially red roses, but chrysanthemums are offered only at funerals! Many in France mark *Toussaints* (All Saints' Day) on November 1 by visiting the cemetery to place chrysanthemums on gravesites.

Vocabulaire

Des Arbres	Trees
un bouleau	birch
une branche	branch
un chêne	oak
un érable	maple
une feuille	leaf
un orme	elm
un peuplier	poplar
un pin	pine tree
un platane	sycamore
un tronc	trunk

Des phénomènes naturels	Natural Phenomena
l'arc-en-ciel	rainbow
l'aube (f.)	sunrise
le brouillard	fog
le coucher du soleil	sunset
un éclair	lightning
la foudre	lightning bolt
une inondation	flood

un orage	thunderstorm
une tempête de neige	snowstorm
le tonnerre	thunder
une tornade	tornado

BRAIN TICKLERS
Set # 52

Fill in the appropriate word from the preceding vocabulary lists.

1. Après l'orage un bel _____ est apparu.

2. Le matin il est parfois difficile de voir à cause du _____.

3. S'il pleut trop, les personnes qui habitent près d'une rivière ont peur d'une _____.

4. Cet arbre a un tronc blanc et gracieux, c'est un ____.

5. Si tu enlèves les pétales une à une d'une _____ tu peux raconter: Il m'aime un peu, beaucoup, pas du tout. (He loves me, he loves me not.)

6. Le premier mai on offre du _____ à ses amis.

(Answers are on page 213.)

Grammaire
Le subjonctif (The Subjunctive)

The subjunctive is a mood rather than a tense. Up to this chapter you have been learning different tenses of the indicative. The indicative mood states facts or certainty and reality. *Il pleut*, It's raining; *Nous sommes allés au ciné*, We went to the movies.

The subjunctive occurs often in French. When it is used in English, most native English speakers are not aware they are using it. For example, when you say, "It's important that she be on time," *Il faut qu'elle soit à l'heure*, the *be* is the subjunctive. You would never say "She be on time" by itself.

The subjunctive occurs when there are **two clauses** and the **two subjects are different**. The first clause expresses emotion, uncertainty, necessity, commands, and opinions. The subject of the first clause is expressing his or her opinions about the action of the second clause.

Il est bon que nous soyons en classe. (It is good that we're in class.) This sounds like a statement a teacher might say. It reflects his or her opinion of the fact that we are in class. A student might say, *Il n'est pas juste que nous soyons en classe*. (It's not fair that we're in class!) Each expresses his or her opinion about the second clause.

The subjunctive is formed by using the *ils* form of the present tense and dropping the *-ent* to form the stem (*ils parlent, parl-*) It will always be inside the *que* clause, so say it with the *que*. The endings to add are *e, es, e, ions, iez,* and *ent*.

-er verbs: *ils travaillent* stem: *travaill-*

Que je travaille	que nous travaillions
Que tu travailles	que vous travailliez
Qu'il travaille	qu'ils travaillent
Qu'elle travaille	qu'elles travaillent

-ir verbs: *il finissent* stem: *finisse-*

Que je finisse	que nous finissions
Que tu finisses	que vous finissiez
Qu'il finisse	qu'ils finissent
Qu'elle finisse	qu'elles finissent

-re verbs: *ils vendent* stem: *vend-*

Que je vende	que nous vendions
Que tu vendes	que vous vendiez
Qu'il vende	qu'ils vendent
Qu'elle vende	qu'elles vendent

Il faut comes from the verb *falloir*, to be necessary. It has only an *il* form. It uses an infinitive or the subjunctive to make the meaning more specific:

> *Il faut rendre les livres à la bibliothèque.* It is necessary to return the books to the library.
> *Il faut que tu rendes les livres à la bibliothèque.* It is necessary that you return the books to the library. (or, You must return . . .)

Proverbe: Didier dit

Il faut oublier et pardonner. Forgive and forget.

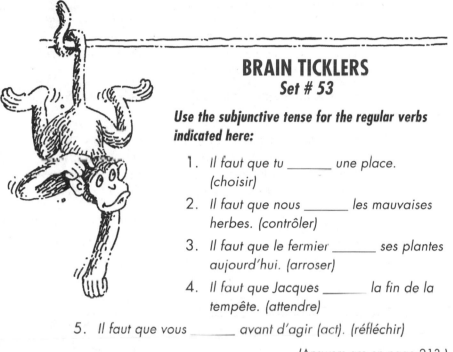

BRAIN TICKLERS
Set # 53

Use the subjunctive tense for the regular verbs indicated here:

1. Il faut que tu _____ une place. (choisir)

2. Il faut que nous _____ les mauvaises herbes. (contrôler)

3. Il faut que le fermier _____ ses plantes aujourd'hui. (arroser)

4. Il faut que Jacques _____ la fin de la tempête. (attendre)

5. Il faut que vous _____ avant d'agir (act). (réfléchir)

(Answers are on page 213.)

Encore c'est mieux

Many expressions require the use of the subjunctive in the clause that follows. Here are some impersonal expressions:

Il est amusant	It is amusing
Il est bon	It is good
Il est dommage	It is too bad
Il est essentiel	It is essential
Il est important	It is important
Il est impossible	It is impossible
Il est injuste	It is unfair
Il est juste	It is fair
Il est nécessaire	It is necessary
Il est utile	It is useful
Il semble	It seems

Often an infinitive is used in English to express the subjunctive:

Il est utile que tu étudies le français. It is useful to study French.

There are many irregular verbs. Study these forms:

Avoir and *être* are unique because their forms do not follow the endings of all the other subjunctive verbs, regular or irrregular.

> ***Avoir* (to have):** *que j'aie, que tu aies, qu'il/elle ait, que nous ayons, que vous ayez, qu'ils/elles aient*
>
> ***Etre* (to be):** *que je sois, que tu sois, qu'il/elle soit, que nous soyons, que vous soyez, qu'ils/elles soient*

These irregular verbs have one stem and use the same endings as regular verbs:

> ***Faire* (to do** or **make):** *que je fasse, que tu fasses, qu'il/elle fasse, que nous fassions, que vous fassiez, qu'ils/elles fassent*
>
> ***Pouvoir* (to be able):** *que je puisse, que tu puisses, qu'il/elle puisse, que nous puissions, que vous puissiez, qu'ils/elles puissent*
>
> ***Pleuvoir* (to rain):** *qu'il pleuve*
>
> ***Savoir* (to know):** *que je sache, que tu saches, qu'il/elle sache, que nous sachions, que vous sachiez, qu'ils/elles sachent*

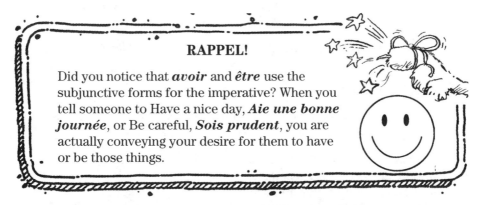

RAPPEL!

Did you notice that *avoir* and *être* use the subjunctive forms for the imperative? When you tell someone to Have a nice day, *Aie une bonne journée*, or Be careful, *Sois prudent*, you are actually conveying your desire for them to have or be those things.

The following verbs use the same endings as the other subjunctive verbs, but have **two stems:** The *ils* form is used as the stem for the *je, tu, il, elle, ils,* and *elles* forms; the *nous* form is used as the stem for the *nous* and *vous* forms.

> ***Boire* (to drink):** *que je boive, que tu boives, qu'il/elle boive, que nous **buvions**, que vous **buviez**, qu'ils/elles boivent*

Croire (**to believe**): *que je croie, que tu croies, qu'il/elle croie, que nous* **croyions**, *que vous* **croyiez**, *qu'ils/elles croient*

Devoir (**to have to**): *que je doive, que tu doives, qu'il/elle doive, que nous* **devions**, *que vous* **deviez**, *qu'ils/elles doivent*

Recevoir (**to receive**): *que je reçoive, que tu reçoives, qu'il/elle reçoive, que nous* **recevions**, *que vous* **receviez**, *qu'ils/elles reçoivent*

Venir (**to come**): *que je vienne, que tu viennes, qu'il/elle vienne, que nous* **venions**, *que vous* **veniez**, *qu'ils/elles viennent*

Voir (**to see**): *que je voie, que tu voies, qu'il/elle voie, que vous* **voyiez**, *que nous* **voyions**, *qu'ils/elles voient*

Stem change verbs follow the same rules as two-stem verbs:

Acheter (**to buy**): *que j'achète, que tu achètes, qu'il/elle achète, que nous* **achetions**, *que vous* **achetiez**, *qu'ils/elles achètent*

Appeler (**to call**): *que j'appelle, que tu appelles, qu'il/elle appelle, que nous* **appelions**, *que vous* **appeliez**, *qu'ils/elles appellent*

Jeter (**to throw**): *que je jette, que tu jettes, qu'il/elle jette, que nous* **jetions**, *que vous* **jetiez**, *qu'ils/elles jettent*

Nettoyer (**to clean**): *que je nettoie, que tu nettoies, qu'il/elle nettoie, que nous* **nettoyions**, *que vous* **nettoyiez**, *qu'ils/elles nettoient*

Préférer (**to prefer**): *que je préfère, que tu préfères, qu'il/elle préfère, que nous* **préférions**, *que vous* **préfériez**, *qu'ils/elles préfèrent*

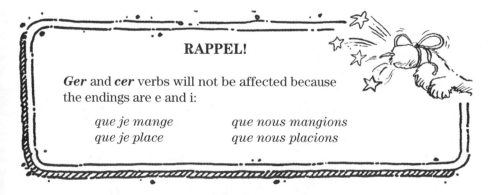

RAPPEL!

Ger and *cer* verbs will not be affected because the endings are e and i:

que je mange	*que nous mangions*
que je place	*que nous placions*

These verbs have two stems and are irregular:

> **Aller** (**to go**): *que j'aille, que tu ailles, qu'il/elle aille, que nous allions, que vous alliez, qu'ils/elles aillent*
> **Vouloir** (**to want**): *que je veuille, que tu veuilles, qu'il/elle veuille, que nous voulions, que vous vouliez, qu'ils/elles veuillent*

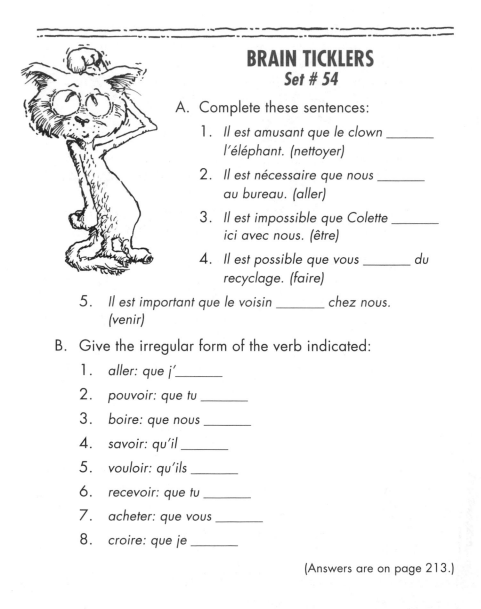

BRAIN TICKLERS
Set # 54

A. Complete these sentences:

1. *Il est amusant que le clown _____ l'éléphant. (nettoyer)*

2. *Il est nécessaire que nous _____ au bureau. (aller)*

3. *Il est impossible que Colette _____ ici avec nous. (être)*

4. *Il est possible que vous _____ du recyclage. (faire)*

5. *Il est important que le voisin _____ chez nous. (venir)*

B. Give the irregular form of the verb indicated:

1. *aller: que j'_____*

2. *pouvoir: que tu _____*

3. *boire: que nous _____*

4. *savoir: qu'il _____*

5. *vouloir: qu'ils _____*

6. *recevoir: que tu _____*

7. *acheter: que vous _____*

8. *croire: que je _____*

(Answers are on page 213.)

Répète après moi!

The i and y in French can catch a speaker of English. Remember that there is no i like *eye* in French; it is always *ee*. It's the same for y. Practice these words that contain the *ee* sound:

> Hypermarché, recycler, myosotis, cybercafé, nylon, lys (pronounce the s)

> (Superstore, recycle, forget-me-not, cybercafé, nylon, lily)

> Nice, iris, science, biologie, nitroglycérine, pieux, icône, Miami, crime

> (Nice, iris, science, biology, nitroglycerine, pious, icon, Miami, crime)

Encore c'est mieux

Here are some other expressions that require the subjunctive. Notice that these express emotion, doubt, demands, desires, and wishing:

aimer	to like	*interdire*	to prohibit
aimer mieux	to prefer	*ordonner*	to order
défendre	to forbid	*préférer*	to prefer
demander	to ask	*souhaiter*	to wish
désirer	to desire	*vouloir*	to want

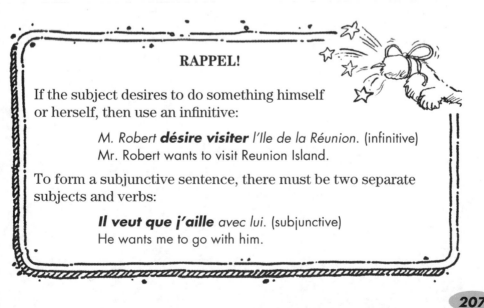

RAPPEL!

If the subject desires to do something himself or herself, then use an infinitive:

> M. Robert **désire visiter** l'Ile de la Réunion. (infinitive)
> Mr. Robert wants to visit Reunion Island.

To form a subjunctive sentence, there must be two separate subjects and verbs:

> **Il veut que j'aille** avec lui. (subjunctive)
> He wants me to go with him.

Grammaire

These expressions of feelings are also followed by an infinitive or subjunctive clause:

Use the **subject + *être* + adjective + *de* + infinitive** for the infinitive structure (when there is only one subject):

> *Je suis heureuse de sortir ce soir.* I am happy to go out tonight.

Use the **subject + *être* + adjective + *que* + second subject + subjunctive** (when there are two separate subjects):

> *Je suis heureuse que tu sortes aussi.* I am happy that you are going out too.

content(e)	happy
déçu(e)	disappointed
désolé(e)	sorry
enchanté(e)	delighted
étonné(e)	surprised
fâché(e)	angry
furieux (furieuse)	furious
heureux (heureuse)	happy
malheureux (malheureuse)	unhappy
ravi(e)	delighted
surpris(e)	surprised
triste	sad
avoir peur	to be afraid
avoir honte	to be ashamed
regretter	to be sorry

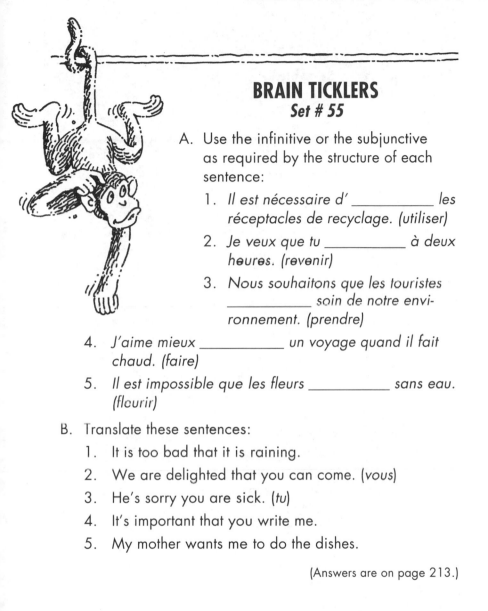

BRAIN TICKLERS
Set # 55

A. Use the infinitive or the subjunctive as required by the structure of each sentence:

1. *Il est nécessaire d'* _____ *les réceptacles de recyclage. (utiliser)*

2. *Je veux que tu* _____ *à deux heures. (revenir)*

3. *Nous souhaitons que les touristes* _____ *soin de notre environnement. (prendre)*

4. *J'aime mieux* _____ *un voyage quand il fait chaud. (faire)*

5. *Il est impossible que les fleurs* _____ *sans eau. (fleurir)*

B. Translate these sentences:

1. It is too bad that it is raining.

2. We are delighted that you can come. (*vous*)

3. He's sorry you are sick. (*tu*)

4. It's important that you write me.

5. My mother wants me to do the dishes.

(Answers are on page 213.)

A réfléchir
Madagascar

Madagascar, or **Republic of Madagascar** (older name **Malagasy Republic**), is an island nation in the Indian Ocean off the southeastern coast of Africa. The main island is the fourth-largest island in the world. The variety of its landscape spans from volcanic mountains to broad plains and even a desert. The myriad forest types provide habitats for its amazing variety of animal species and plants—over 150,000 that only exist on Madagascar. The most famous of all is the lemur, of which there are 100 varieties. They and other species of birds and reptiles are unique to Madagascar as a result of the island drifting away from Africa 160 million years ago; there were no predators to endanger them before man arrived on the scene. The wildlife of Madagascar is an attraction to tourists, and tourism is the main industry of the island. A national effort to protect the habitat of these unique animals is a priority of the Malagasy government. The national language is Malagasy. Early inhabitants were Indonesian, African, Asian, and Middle Eastern. Arabs first established trading posts around the year 800, and various nationalities arrived over the years. From 1600 to 1700 pirates used Madagascar as a favorite hideout. In 1817 slavery was abolished under English rule. The French invaded Madagascar in 1883, and Madagascar was a colony of France until it obtained its independence in 1960. The primary exports are vanilla, coffee, sugar, and shellfish. If you would like to know more about Madagascar's wildlife, check out *www.wildmadagascar.org.*

Tu sais quoi?

Madagascar is the leading world producer of vanilla. The bean is actually produced by an orchid that is pollinated by hand. It is one of the world's most labor-intensive and therefore expensive spices. It was originally grown in Mexico, and the Mayans even used it for currency. Cortés discovered it in 1519 and brought it back to Europe. From there cultivation spread to various countries, including Guatemala, Tahiti, the Philippines, and China. There are eight stages of preparation before the bean is ready for sale. When the bean is harvested it is green and odorless. It is then boiled, cured, and stored before being graded for quality and packed for shipment. The scent of vanilla is a natural calmative and a popular perfume fragrance.

Jean-Jacques Rousseau was born in 1712 in Geneva, Switzerland. He was the son of a clock maker, and his mother died while he was young. He was placed under the tutelage of Madame de Warens, who encouraged him to study music. He knew the great philosophers of his time, such as Diderot and Voltaire. He was passionate about botany and wrote *Lettres sur la botanique* to help one of his friend's daughters to better understand plant classifications. He admired natural gardens and was ahead of his time in his field. He wrote that men were born naturally good and that society corrupted them; his essential doctrine emphasized a return to nature and the natural. In *La Nouvelle Héloïse* he writes of the value of a natural garden where nothing is planted in a balanced, forced design. This was a great departure from the popular French gardens of his time designed by André le Nôtre at Versailles.

La Nouvelle Héloïse, 4e partie, livre XI (an extract)

Vous ne voyez rien d'aligné, rien de nivelé; jamais un cordeau n'entra dans ce lieu; la nature ne plante rien au cordeau... Tout ce que vous voyez sont des plantes sauvages ou robustes qu'il suffit de mettre en terre, et qui viennent ensuite d'elles-mêmes. D'ailleurs la nature semble dérober aux yeux des hommes ses vrais attraits, auxquels ils semblent trop peu sensibles, et qu'ils défigurent quand ils sont à leur portée; elle fuit les lieux fréquentés; c'est au sommet des montagnes, au fond des forêts, dans les îles désertes qu'elle étale ses charmes les plus touchants.
www.rousseau-2012.fr/connaitre-rousseau/

Amis/Faux Amis

Did you notice these *faux amis*?

> *Défendre* means "to forbid," not defend; and *demander* means to "ask for," not demand.
> *L'herbe* means "grass" in French as well as herbs for flavoring.
> *Sable* means "sand" in French.
> *Un castor* is a beaver, not the roller on a chair leg.
> *Une source* is a spring (water).
> *Un champ* refers to a field, not the champion.

BRAIN TICKLERS — THE ANSWERS

Set # 50, page 195

A.

1. *une mouffette*
2. *une source*
3. *un île*
4. *une coccinelle*
5. *un faucon*
6. *une colline*
7. *un moineau*
8. *une alouette*
9. *un papillon*
10. *un chêne*

B.
Answers will vary.

C.
See text.

Set # 51, page 198

A.

1. *Ne touche pas*
2. *Photographiez*
3. *Ne donnez pas*
4. *Faisons*
5. *Ne coupe pas*

B.

1. *champ/field*
2. *source/spring*
3. *chenille/caterpillar*
4. *geai bleu/blue jay*
5. *mouffette/skunk*

Set #52, page 201

1. *arc-en-ciel*
2. *brouillard*
3. *inondation*
4. *bouleau*
5. *marguerite*
6. *muguet*

Set # 53, page 203

1. *choisisses*
2. *contrôlions*
3. *arrose*
4. *attende*
5. *réfléchissiez*

Set # 54, page 206

A.

1. *nettoie*
2. *allions*
3. *soit*
4. *fassiez*
5. *vienne*

B.

1. *aille*
2. *puisses*
3. *buvions*
4. *sache*

5. *veuillent*
6. *reçoives*
7. *achetiez*
8. *croie*

Set # 55, page 209

A.

1. *utiliser*
2. *reviennes*
3. *prennent*
4. *faire*
5. *fleurissent*

B.

1. *Il est dommage qu'il pleuve.*
2. *Nous sommes ravis que vous puissiez venir.*
3. *Il regrette* (or *il est désolé*) *que tu sois malade.*
4. *Il est important que tu m'écrives.*
5. *Ma mère veut que je fasse la vaisselle.*

J'aime m'enrichir:
La littérature et les arts

I LIKE TO BROADEN MY HORIZONS: LITERATURE AND THE ARTS

Salut! C'est Sophie. Que fais-tu le week-end? Moi, j'aime accompagner mes parents à un musée pour voir de l'art. J'aime regarder les peintures, les sculptures, et les expositions. J'ai de la chance d'habiter à Paris où il y a tant de musées. J'aime les peintures impressionnistes qu'on peut voir au Musée d'Orsay. Peut-être tu connais Claude Monet, Auguste Renoir, ou Edouard Manet? Ils sont très célèbres, mais il y en a beaucoup d'autres, comme Vincent van Gogh, Paul Cézanne, Edgar Degas, et Marie Cassatt. Il y a des peintures en huile, des aquarelles, des dessins en fusain, des pastels, et des gravures. J'aime les peintures de la nature ou les paysages, mais les portraits et les natures mortes sont aussi intéressants. Le Musée d'Orsay était une gare et on l'a presque démolie avant de le faire un musée. Dans le musée, on trouve une boutique, une salle de bal orné, un restaurant, et même un café en haut. Parfois nous allons au Musée du Louvre avec la classe. Quand nous avons étudié l'Egypte ancien, nous sommes allés voir les trésors des pyramides avec des momies. Bien sûr la peinture la plus célèbre du monde, la Joconde (Mona Lisa en anglais) est au Musée du Louvre. Léonard da Vinci avait peint la Joconde en Italie avant de l'apporter en France. Jean-Luc aime l'art moderne, et de temps en temps il m'emmène au Centre Pompidou. Là nous explorons les salles d'art du vingtième siècle et des œuvres de notre époque. Il y a toutes sortes de choses à voir et il y a des films aussi. Puisque nous sommes élèves, la visite des musées nationaux est gratuite.

Vocabulaire	
Au musée	**Museum**
une aquarelle	watercolor
un dessin en fusain	charcoal drawing
une exposition	exhibit
une gravure	engraving

une momie	mummy
un musée	museum
une nature morte	still life
un pastel	pastel drawing
un paysage	landscape
un peintre	painter
une peinture	painting
un portrait	portrait
une salle de bal	ballroom
un sculpteur	sculptor
une sculpture	sculpture
un trésor	treasure

Spectacles — Shows

acteur (actrice)	actor /actress
un balcon	balcony
un ballet	ballet
un billet	ticket
un cascadeur	stuntman

une comédie	a play with a happy ending/ contrast with tragedy
comédien (comédienne)	actor/actress
danseur (danseuse)	dancer
un fauteuil d'orchestre	orchestra seat
un guichet	ticket booth
un opéra	opera
un orchestre	orchestra
une pièce de théâtre	play

une place	seat
un rang	row
un rideau	curtain
le texte	lines
un théâtre	theater
une tragédie	a tragedy
la vedette	star

Proverbe: Didier dit

Beaucoup de bruit pour rien. Much ado about nothing.
(Literally: A lot of noise for nothing.)

Vocabulaire

Le Cinéma	Movies
genres de films	types of movies
une comédie	comedy
un dessin animé	cartoon
un documentaire	documentary
un film d'amour	love story
un film d'aventures	adventure film
un film d'espionnage	spy story
un film policier	police story
un western	western
un film de guerre	war story
un film d'horreur	horror film
un film de science fiction	science fiction film

Miscellanées	Miscellaneous
applaudir	to applaud
entrer en scène	to come on stage
frapper les trois coups	Traditional French way of starting a play: three loud knocks
huer	to boo
jouer un rôle	to play a character
répéter	to rehearse
réserver	to book
siffler	to whistle
sortir de scène	to exit the stage

 **Vive la différence!**

Don't whistle if you like a performance or a performer. In France, a loud whistle has the opposite meaning. If you whistle loudly with enthusiasm, it is the equivalent of booing at the stage!

BRAIN TICKLERS
Set # 56

A. Match the art terms:

1. ___ un dessin   a. painting
2. ___ un sculpteur   b. painter
3. ___ un paysage   c. drawing
4. ___ un peintre   d. still life
5. ___ une gravure   e. sculptor
6. ___ une nature morte   f. landscape
7. ___ une peinture   g. engraving
                     h. sculpture

B. Name a movie you have seen for each of the following:

1. *un film d'horreur:*_____
2. *un film de science fiction:* _____
3. *un film d'amour:*_____
4. *un film de guerre:*_____
5. *un film d'aventures:*_____

(Answers are on page 236.)

Grammaire
Le plus-que-parfait, le conditionnel passé, et le futur antérieur (The Pluperfect, the Past Conditional, and the Future Perfect)

In this chapter you will learn three compound tenses. They follow the same rules as the passé composé: Most verbs use *avoir* as the helping verb, and about 16 use *être*, the Dr. and Mrs. Vandertramp verbs (see p. 62). Reflexive verbs use *être* too. These tenses also follow the same rules for agreement of past participles.

Grammaire
Le plus-que-parfait

Le plus-que-parfait is formed by combining the imperfect of the helping verb (*avoir* or *être*) and the past participle. The pluperfect is a past tense that precedes another past action.

Sample Conjugations Using *avoir*, *être*, and Reflexive Verbs
Imperfect + past participle:

Visiter to visit

J'avais visité	*Nous avions visité*
Tu avais visité	*Vous aviez visité*
Il avait visité	*Ils avaient visité*
Elle avait visité	*Elles avaient visité*

J'**avais** déjà **visité** le Louvre quand tu es arrivé à Paris.
I had already visited the Louvre when you arrived in Paris.

Sortir to go out

J'étais sorti(e)	*Nous étions sortis(es)*
Tu étais sorti(e)	*Vous étiez sorti(e)(s)(es)*
Il était sorti	*Ils étaient sortis*
Elle était sortie	*Elles étaient sorties*

Tu **étais** déjà **sortie** quand je t'ai téléphoné.
You had already gone out when I called you.

Se lever to get up

Je m'étais levé(e)	*Nous nous étions levés(es)*
Tu t'étais levé(e)	*Vous vous étiez levé(e)(s)(es)*
Il s'était levé	*Ils s'étaient levés*
Elle s'était levée	*Elles s'étaient levées*

Il **s'était** déjà **levé** quand le réveil a sonné.
He had already gotten up when the alarm rang.

Negation

Je ne **m'étais** pas **couché** avant toi. I hadn't gone to bed
before you.

Ils **n'avaient** jamais **mangé** du pâté. They had never
eaten paté before.

Inversion

Aviez-vous jamais **vu** un lemur avant d'aller au zoo? Had
you ever seen a lemur before going to the zoo?

N'étais-tu pas **parti** quand ton père s'est réveillé? Hadn't
you left when your father woke up?

Ne nous **étions**-nous pas **rencontrés** l'année passée?
Hadn't we met last year?

Booz endormi

Booz s'était couché de fatigue accablé;
Il avait tout le jour travaillé dans son aire;
Puis avait fait son lit à sa place ordinaire;
Booz dormait auprès des boisseaux pleins de blé.

—*Victor Hugo*

Vocabulaire

accablé	overwhelmed
aire	threshing floor
boisseaux	bushels
plein	full
blé	wheat

BRAIN TICKLERS
Set # 57

A. Rewrite these sentences in the plus-que-parfait:

1. *Nous sommes allés à la pièce* Les Misérables *l'année dernière.*
2. *Qui a ouvert la porte?*
3. *Pierre n'a pas aimé le film d'amour.*
4. *Les enfants ont peint des paysages.*
5. *Le professeur est monté au premier étage pour voir la Joconde.*

B. Write five sentences about things you did by the time you were six years old.

Ex: *J'avais appris à parler anglais.*

(Answers are on page 236.)

Grammaire
Le conditionnel passé

The past conditional tense is formed by combining the conditional tense of the helping verb and the past participle of the main verb. It is most often used with the **plus-que-parfait** in "if" clauses using *si*.

> Si ***j'étais allé*** *au théâtre avec toi,* ***j'aurais vu*** *la pièce.*
> If I had gone (plus-que-parfait) to the theater with you, I would have seen (conditionnel passé) the play.

Conditional Tense + the Past Participle
Sample conjugations using *avoir*, *être*, and reflexive verbs:

Voir to see

J'aurais vu	*Nous aurions vu*
Tu aurais vu	*Vous auriez vu*
Il aurait vu	*Ils auraient vu*
Elle aurait vu	*Elles auraient vu*

*Si tu étais arrivé à l'heure, tu **aurais vu** la vedette.*
If you had arrived on time, you **would have seen** the star.

Sortir to go out

Je serais sorti(e)	*Nous serions sortis(es)*
Tu serais sorti(e)	*Vous seriez sorti(e)(s)(es)*
Il serait sorti	*Ils seraient sortis*
Elle serait sortie	*Elles seraient sorties*

*Si tu l'avais invitée, elle **serait sortie**.*
If you had invited her, **she would have gone out**.

Se coucher to go to bed

Je me serais couché(e)	*Nous nous serions couchés(es)*
Tu te serais couché(e)	*Vous vous seriez couché(e)(s)(es)*
Ils se serait couché	*Ils se seraient couchés*
Elle se serait couchée	*Elles se seraient couchées*

*Il se **serait couché** s'il avait été fatigué.*
He **would have gone to bed** if he had been tired.

BRAIN TICKLERS
Set # 58

A. Write these sentences in the past conditional:

1. *Tu _____ le documentaire sur les pingouins. (aimer)*

2. *L'actrice principale _____ en scène si elle n'avait pas oublié son texte. (entrer)*

3. *Vous _____ au théâtre de l'Absurde. (s'amuser)*

4. *Les acteurs _____ célèbre, si le film avait réussi. (être)*

5. *Nous _____ si la comédie avait été drôle. (applaudir)*

B. Write original clauses with the past conditional to complete the idea:

1. *S'il avait neigé . . .*

2. *Si nous avions voulu . . .*

3. *Si j'avais le temps . . .*

4. *Si j'avais gagné la lotérie . . .*

(Answers are on page 237.)

Vocabulaire: Encore c'est mieux

Littérature	Literature
un auteur	author
une autobiographie	autobiography
une biographie	biography
un conte de fée	fairy tale
un/une correspondant/e	pen pal
une bande dessinée	comic strip
un écrivain	writer
un éditeur	publisher
un/une lecteur/lectrice	reader
un livre de poche	paperback
un poème	poem
la poésie	poetry
un poète	poet
un roman d'amour	love story
un roman de science fiction	science fiction novel
un/une romancier/romancière	novelist
un roman d'espionnage	spy novel
un roman d'intrigue	mystery
un roman policier	detective novel
un vers	line, verse

Des verbes	Some Useful Verbs
citer	to quote
correspondre	to correspond
écrire	to write
imprimer	to print
lire	to read
publier	to publish
rimer	to rhyme

La Musique	Music
un/une chanteur/chanteuse	singer
composer	to compose
un compositeur	composer
un concert	concert
une salle de musique	concert hall
interpréter	to interpret
le jazz	jazz
jouer d'un instrument	to play an instrument
un/une musicien(ne)	musician
la musique africaine	African music
la musique classique	classical music
la musique folklorique	folk music
une ouverture	overture
les paroles	lyrics
le rap	rap music
le rock	rock music
les spectateurs	audience

Les Instruments	Instruments
un accordéon	accordion
une clarinette	clarinet
un clavier	keyboard
des cymbales (f.)	cymbals
une flûte	flute
une flûte à bec	recorder
une guitare	guitar
un hautbois	oboe
un saxophone	saxophone
un trombone	trombone
une trompette	trumpet
un violon	violin
un violoncelle	cello

 **Vive la différence!**

La gamme: The scale in French is almost the same as in English. Can you spot the difference? do (C), ré (D), mi (E), fa (F), sol (G), la (A), si (B).

Bémol stands for flat and *dièse* is sharp.

Answer: si (B) is ti in English!

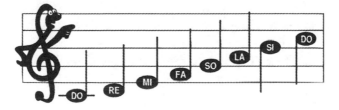

Grammaire
Le futur antérieur

This tense is formed by using the future of the helping verb *avoir* or *être* and the past participle of the main verb. It implies an action in the future that will precede or occur before another future event or action:

> Je **serai parti(e)** avant la fin de l'été.
> I **will have left** before the end of summer.

Future of Helping Verb + Past Participle

> J'**aurai fini** le roman d'espionnage avant de voir le film.
> I **will have finished** the spy novel before seeing the movie.

Sample conjugations using *avoir*, *être*, and reflexive verbs:

Finir to finish; I will have finished

J'aurai fini	Nous aurons fini
Tu auras fini	Vous aurez fini
Il aura fini	Ils auront fini
Elle aura fini	Elles auront fini

Arriver to arrive

Je serai arrivé(e)	Nous serons arrivé(e)s
Tu seras arrivé(e)	Vous serez arrivé(e)(s)
Il sera arrivé	Ils seront arrivés
Elle sera arrivé(e)	Elles seront arrivées

> Je **serai arrivé** quand tu téléphoneras.
> I **will have arrived** when you telephone.

Se coucher to go to bed

Je me serai couché(e)	Nous nous serons couché(e)s
Tu te seras couché(e)	Vous vous serez couché(e)(s)
Il se sera couché	Ils se seront couchés
Elle se sera couchée	Elles se seront couchées

> Je **me serai couché** quand mes parents rentreront de l'opéra.
> I **will have gone to bed** when my parents come home from the opera.

Proverbe: Didier dit

C'est le ton qui fait la musique. It's not what you say but how you say it. (Literally: It's the tone that makes the music.)

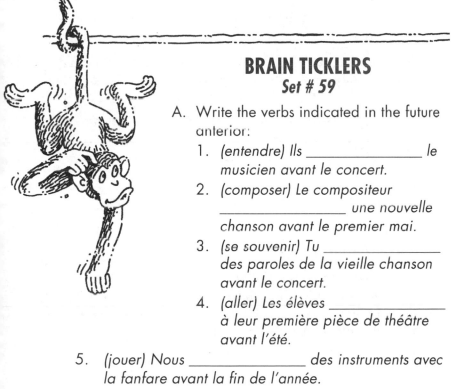

BRAIN TICKLERS
Set # 59

A. Write the verbs indicated in the future anterior:

1. *(entendre)* Ils _____ le musicien avant le concert.
2. *(composer)* Le compositeur _____ une nouvelle chanson avant le premier mai.
3. *(se souvenir)* Tu _____ des paroles de la vieille chanson avant le concert.
4. *(aller)* Les élèves _____ à leur première pièce de théâtre avant l'été.
5. *(jouer)* Nous _____ des instruments avec la fanfare avant la fin de l'année.

B. *Vocabulaire: littérature:* Translate the following sentences into French.

By next summer, *Avant l'été prochain* . . .

1. The writer will have written a detective novel.
2. The poet will have finished his love poem.
3. The journalist will have corresponded with the president.
4. The publisher will have published the cartoon.
5. I will have read a fairy tale.

(Answers are on page 237.)

Répète après moi!

The letter o has two pronunciations. If it is the final vowel sound or has a circumflex over it, it is a long o like *oh*: Pronounce these words with the long *oh* sound:

> *bientôt, piano, chose, Miro, saxo, trop, sirop, resto, micro, chômage*
> (soon, piano, thing, Miro [painter], saxophone, too much, syrup, short for restaurant, microphone, unemployment)

The short o like the o in "mother" occurs generally when it is followed by another syllable or a pronounced final consonant sound:

> *violon, sommeil, chronique, robe, folle, collier, opéra, roman, correspondre, comédie, le rock, coq, choc*
> (violin, sleepy, chronic, dress, crazy, necklace, opera, novel, to correspond, comedy, rock music, rooster, shock)

Grammaire
Savoir et Connaître: Two verbs to "know"

In French there are two ways of knowing something or someone.
  Savoir means to know a fact: a number or a clause containing a fact, how to do something when it is followed by an infinitive, or *savoir* can stand alone.

Savoir

Je sais	*Nous savons*
Tu sais	*Vous savez*
Il/elle sait	*Ils/elles savent*

Passé composé: *j'ai su*
Future tense: *je saurai*

Savoir: to know a fact, how to do something

> *Je sais **ton numéro de** téléphone et ton adresse.*
> I know your phone number and address (facts).

Je sais **à quelle heure la pièce commence**. I know
what time the play begins.

Je sais **danser** le tango. I know how to dance the tango.

Sais-tu **qu'il pleut**? Oui, je **sais**! Do you know it's raining?
Yes, I know!

Connaître means to know or be acquainted with a person or
place. It implies that your knowledge is multifaceted: You know
your friend's parents, what they look like, how they dress, what
they wear, and so on.

When *connaître* is used, it must have a noun or pronoun with it.

Try substituting the idea "to be acquainted or familiar" to
decide which verb to use.

The verb form must be used with a person, place, or object
of acquaintance:

Je connais **tes parents**. Je les connais depuis cinq ans.
I know your parents. I've known them for five years.

Je connais bien **ma ville**. Je sais le code postal.
I know (am familiar with) my town. I know the zip code.
(factual)

Je connais **les peintures de Cézanne**.
I am familiar with the paintings of Cézanne.

Connaître: to know, be acquainted

Je connais	Nous connaissons
Tu connais	Vous connaissez
Il/elle connaît	Ils/elles connaissent

Passé composé: *j'ai connu*
Future tense: *je connaîtrai*

Expressions with *savoir* and *connaître*

savoir-faire	ability, know-how
savoir-vivre	tact or good manners
un certain je ne sais quoi	there is something rather vague
Dieu sait comment	Heaven only knows
connaisseur	connoisseur, expert
perdre connaissance	to lose consciousness
faire la connaissance de	to make someone's acquaintance

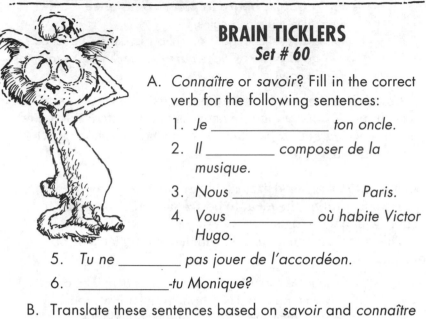

BRAIN TICKLERS
Set # 60

A. *Connaître* or *savoir*? Fill in the correct verb for the following sentences:

1. *Je* _____ *ton oncle.*
2. *Il* _____ *composer de la musique.*
3. *Nous* _____ *Paris.*
4. *Vous* _____ *où habite Victor Hugo.*
5. *Tu ne* _____ *pas jouer de l'accordéon.*
6. _____-*tu Monique?*

B. Translate these sentences based on *savoir* and *connaître* and their expressions.

1. She lost consciousness.
2. We will know how to speak French.
3. I know where Tahiti is located.
4. We know our teacher well.
5. Mr. Smith is an art connoisseur.

(Answers are on page 237.)

Info

Les Impresssionistes. Claude Monet, Auguste Renoir, Edouard Manet, Edgar Degas, Berthe Morisot, and Camille Pissaro were some of the artists involved with the art movement known as impressionism. Late in the nineteenth century, these artists took their painting outside to capture the effects of light. Paintings of landscapes, waterscapes, and city scenes were painted under all weather conditions. Black and gray

were banished from their palettes as these artists experimented with colors applied quickly yet in a calculated manner to capture the shadows and highlights of the moment. At that time established art critics scorned the painters. Monet's painting of a sunrise, *Lever du soleil: Impression*, provided the origin of the term *impressionism*. Today the paintings of the period are very valuable and popular. You can see many of them online or in museums throughout the world. Try a virtual visit to the Musée d'Orsay where you can see pre- and postimpressionist paintings as well, at *www.musee-orsay.fr*.

Tahiti, Pearl of the Pacific

Tahiti is the largest of the Polynesian islands. It is made up of two islands, Tahiti Nui (*la grande île*) and Tahiti Iti. Polynesians first landed their large canoes in Tahiti in about 500 BC. The expeditions of Magellan and Cook and even the famous ship *The Bounty* landed in Tahiti. The French have ruled Tahiti since 1880, and its population speaks both French and Rei na'ohi, the local Tahitian language. The inhabitants of Tahiti are considered French citizens because Tahiti is a semiautonomous French territory. The population is approximately 287,000, consisting mainly of Polynesians. Although the country is quite modern, the traditional warm Polynesian welcome, accompanied by fragrant flower necklaces and songs, still exists. It is an environmental paradise full of a rich variety of exotic fruits, birds, and flowers. There are very few insects and no reptiles or dangerous animals. Favorite meals include fruit from the bread tree, or *l'arbre à pain*, and fresh grilled fish. The waters around Tahiti have been called the richest aquarium in the world. Tourism and the legendary black pearl, found in the lagoons around Tahiti, are two of the most important industries.

Tu sais quoi?
Paul Gauguin

Paul Gauguin was born in 1848 and died in 1903. His parents died when he was young and he worked as a sailor for six years. He then lived with a wealthy guardian who was an art connoisseur. Gauguin learned to appreciate art and to try his hand at painting. He became a banker and then a successful stockbroker. He was very moved by the impressionist paintings he saw at an exhibit. His passion led him to purchase enough impressionist paintings to later finance his move to the Pacific. He decided to become a painter and left his family and former life to spend a period in Arles, France, with Vincent van Gogh, then eventually moved to Panama, Martinique, and finally the sunny Pacific island of Tahiti. He spent the rest of his life painting Tahitians and their countryside. He lived in rustic conditions alongside the natives. Gauguin used colors to express emotion in surprising combinations. He was one of the first artists to use symbolism and abstract art to provoke spiritual meaning. Some of his paintings include *The Yellow Christ (Le Christ jaune)*, *Self-Portrait with Halo (Auto-portrait avec un halo)*, and *Woman with a Flower (Femme avec une fleur)*. www.ibiblio.org/um/paint/auth/gaugin.

Une Carte Postale de Tahiti

Salut Sylvie!

Je t'écris de Papeete en Tahiti. C'est la capitale de la Polynésie française. Quelle belle ville! Hier ma famille et moi avons eu l'occasion de faire une excursion sur l'Océan Pacifique pour chercher des baleines à bosses. Nous en avons aperçu une douzaine aussi bien que des dauphins. C'est une Zone Economique Exclusive—ce qui veut dire que c'est un sanctuaire aquatique où les 800 espèces de poissons, les tortues, et les Raies Manta sont protégés des pêcheurs. Ce matin nous allons visiter le marché Papeete et le parc Bougainville. Pendant la fin du mois de juin jusqu'à la fin de juillet, les Tahitiens célèbrent la fête Heiva. C'est un grand concours d'arts traditionnels. Cet après-midi il va y avoir des concours de pirogue. C'est une sorte d'énorme canoë avec seize rameurs. Après il va y avoir des concours de lancer des javelots vers un noix de coco suspendu en l'air. Ce soir nous allons assister aux concours de danses et de chants traditionnels. Il y a même une compétition des danseurs du feu. Je t'enverrai des photos. Un jour tu devrais venir visiter cette île magique!

A bientôt, Jérôme

Vocabulaire

une baleine à bosse	humpback whale
un dauphin	dolphin
des espèces	species
une tortue	turtle
une raie manta	stingray
un concours	competition
un rameur	rower
un javelot	javelin
un danseur du feu	fire dancer

BRAIN TICKLERS
Set # 61

A. Mark if the following sentences are *vrai* or *faux*, and correct the false statements:

1. *Le Tahiti se trouve dans l'Océan Atlantique.*
2. *Les baleines à bosses ont disparu de cette région.*
3. *Heiva est une fête célébrée en janvier.*
4. *On lance des noix de cocos aussi loin que possible.*
5. *Tahiti se trouve dans une ZEE, une zone protégée.*

B. Give the vocabulary words in French:
1. coconut
2. fire dancer
3. dolphin
4. rower
5. javelin

(Answers are on page 237.)

Amis/Faux Amis

You probably recognized many *amis* in the vocabulary of this chapter: *orchestre, sculpteur, musée, musicien* are a few examples. But note the following *faux amis:*

Un lecteur, une lectrice is a reader.

Une pièce is a play in the theater.

Les spectacteurs are the audience; the word *audience* in French refers to a personal meeting with an important person, for example, an audience with the king.

Un/une comédien/ienne refers to an actor, not to a comedian in the English sense.

Répéter means to rehearse.

BRAIN TICKLERS—THE ANSWERS

Set # 56, page 220

A.
1. c
2. e
3. f
4. b
5. g
6. d
7. a

B.
Answers will vary.

Set # 57, page 223

A.
1. *Nous étions allés à la pièce* Les Misérables *l'année dernière.*
2. *Qui avait ouvert la porte?*
3. *Pierre n'avait pas aimé le film d'amour.*
4. *Les enfants avaient peint des paysages.*
5. *Le professeur était monté au premier étage pour voir la Joconde.*

B.
Answers will vary.

Set # 58, page 224

A.
1. *aurais aimé*
2. *serait entrée*
3. *vous seriez amusé*
4. *auraient été*
5. *aurions applaudi*

B. Sample answers:
1. *j'aurais fait du ski.*
2. *nous serions allés au cirque.*
3. *je serais resté plus long-temps.*
4. *j'aurais acheté une nou-velle voiture pour mes parents.*

Set # 59, page 229

A.
1. *auront entendu*
2. *aura composé*
3. *te seras souvenu*
4. *seront allés*
5. *aurons joué*

B.
1. *L'écrivain aura écrit un roman policier.*
2. *Le poète aura fini son poème d'amour.*
3. *Le journaliste aura corre-spondu avec le président.*
4. *L'éditeur aura publié la bande dessinée.*
5. *J'aurai lu un conte de fée.*

Set # 60, page 232

A.
1. *connais*
2. *sait*
3. *connaissons*
4. *savez*
5. *sais*
6. *Connais*

B.
1. *Elle a perdu connaissance.*
2. *Nous saurons parler français.*
3. *Je sais où se trouve Tahiti.*
4. *Nous connaissons bien notre professeur.*
5. *M. Smith est un connais-seur d'art.*

Set # 61, page 235

A.
1. *faux; l'Océan Pacifique*
2. *faux; Ils n'ont pas disparu.*
3. *faux; en juin et en juillet*
4. *faux; on lance des javelots vers un noix de coco*
5. *vrai*

B.
1. *un noix de coco*
2. *un danseur du feu*
3. *un dauphin*
4. *un rameur*
5. *un javelot*

J'explore le monde francophone

I DISCOVER THE FRENCH-SPEAKING WORLD

Salut! C'est Sophie.

Comme tu as vu, le français est parlé un peu partout dans le monde. Pourquoi y a-t-il tellement de pays et de régions francophones? C'est parce que les explorateurs du seizième siècle jusqu'aux ceux de dix-neuvième siècle ont colonisé autant de pays que possible! Ainsi ils pouvaient importer et vendre les denrées des pays étrangers riches en produits pour vendre en Europe. En Amérique du Nord sont arrivés Jacques Cartier en 1534 et Samuel de Champlain en 1608, des explorateurs du fleuve Saint Laurent, Jacques Marquette et Louis Joliet qui ont exploré le fleuve Mississippi en 1673, et La Salle qui a nommé Louisiane en l'honneur de Louis XIV en 1681. Louis-Antoine de Bougainville, qu'on considère le premier Français de faire le tour du monde in 1766, a exploré la Polynésie et la Mélanésie. Pierre Savorgnan de Brazza, qui était un explorateur italien (naturalisé français), a ouvert les explorations et colonisation de l'Afrique équatoriale. Aujourd'hui la France essaie de maintenir de bonnes relations diplomatiques et économiques avec ses anciennes colonies. Ce qui restent des colonies ont de relations variées avec la France: la Guadeloupe, la Martinique, la Réunion et la Guyane française; les îles Wallis et Futuna, la Nouvelle-Calédonie, la Polynésie française et les Terres australes et antarctiques françaises; Mayotte et Saint-Pierre-et-Miquelon. Si tu veux en savoir plus chercher la liste d'explorateurs français sur l'Internet.

A bientôt, Sophie

Voir aussi: *www.outre-mer.gouv.fr/*

Vocabulaire	
La politique	**Politics**
une ambassade	embassy
un ambassadeur	ambassador
une armée	army

un capitaine	captain
un/une citoyen/ne	citizen
une colonie	colony
une démocratie	democracy
des denrées (f.)	products
une dictature	dictatorship
les droits	rights
une économie	economy
une expédition	expedition
une frontière	border
un gouverneur	governor
une guerre	war
la liberté	freedom
un maire	mayor
une monarchie	monarchy
un navire	ship
un parti	political party
un président	president
une rébellion	rebellion
une reine	queen
une république	republic
une révolution	revolution
un roi	king
un sénat	senate
un traité	treaty
Des verbes	**Verbs**
abolir	to abolish
atterrir	to land

dissoudre	to dissolve
élire	to elect
manifester	to demonstrate
maintenir	to maintain
régner	to rule
se révolter	to revolt
voter	to vote
Miscellanés	**Miscellaneous**
ancien	former (when written in front of the noun)
naturalisé	naturalized
diplomatique	diplomatic
ceux	those
outre-mer	overseas
le tour du monde	journey around the world

Grammaire
Des pronoms relatifs (Relative Pronouns)
Qui and Que

Did you notice that Sophie used *qui* and *que* in the middle of a sentence? In these situations they are relative pronouns.

Relative pronouns are used to introduce clauses that modify or provide additional information about nouns:

> *Jacques Marquette et Louis Joliet,* **qui** *ont exploré le fleuve Mississippi en 1673 . . .*
>
> Jacques Marquette and Louis Joliet, who explored the Mississippi in 1673 . . .
>
> *Louis-Antoine de Bougainville,* **qu**'*on considère le premier Français de faire le tour du monde in 1766 . . .*
>
> Louis-Antoine de Bougainville, who is considered the first Frenchman to complete a trip around the world in 1766 . . .

Qui and *que* are used to introduce relative clauses, and both can mean **who, whom, which,** or **that.** The choice you make depends on their function in the clause. **Qui** replaces the subject of the clause and a verb will follow it. **Que** (**qu'** in front of a vowel) replaces the object of the clause and a noun will follow it.

*C'était Bougainville **qui** a exploré Tahiti.*
It was Bougainville who explored Tahiti.
*Le Bougainvillier est une fleur **qui** sent bon.*
The bougainvillea is a flower that smells good.
*C'est un homme **que** tout le monde admire.*
He's a man that everyone admires.
*Il y a une fleur **qu**'on a nommé Bougainvillier en son honneur.*
There is a flower that was named bougainvillea in his honor.

BRAIN TICKLERS
Set # 62

A. Unscramble the vocabulary terms:

   1. *tdspriéne*   (head of state)

   2. *trove*   (action of election)

   3. *ameré*   (group of soldiers)

   4. *labiro*   (to end something)

   5. *nirtniame*   (to keep in good shape)

B. Fill in **qui** or **que** (**qu'**) as needed:

   1. *Voici une colonie _____ était gouvernée par les français.*

2. *C'est un président _____ on admire.*

3. *Les Etats-Unis a un gouvernement _____ est une démocratie.*

4. *L'ambassade américaine se trouve dans un beau bâtiment _____ n'est pas loin de la Place de la Concorde.*

5. *Brazza était un explorateur _____ les gens trouvaient gentil.*

(Answers are on page 260.)

Proverbes: Didier dit

L'un meurt dont l'autre vit.
One man's poison is another man's meat.
(Literally: One man dies of that by which another man lives.)

Grammaire
Autres Pronoms Relatifs (Other Relative Pronouns)

Dont is used to refer to people or things and means **whose**, of/about **whom, which**.

If the expression calls for **de** when it is written out, the relative clause will be introduced by **dont**.

> *J'ai besoin **du stylo**. Voici le stylo **dont** tu as besoin.*
> I need the pen. Here's the pen you need. (literally, of which you have need)
> *J'ai peur **du chat**. C'est un chat féroce **dont** j'ai peur.*
> I'm afraid of the cat. He's a ferocious cat that I'm afraid of.
> *J'ai vu le film français **dont** tu as parlé.*
> I saw the French film that you talked about. (about which)

Other Uses
When referring to family members you may use:

> *Je connais une fille **dont** la mère est actrice.*
> I know a girl **whose** mother is an actress.
> *Nous parlons au garçon **dont** le père est mon ancien prof.*
> We are talking to the boy **whose** father is my former teacher.

Dont is used only when it directly follows the antecedent it refers to or describes. In the preceding sentences, *dont* follows *stylo, chat, féroce, film français, fille,* and *garçon*.

Other Relative Clauses
Qui
When *qui* is used in a prepositional phrase, it can refer only to people.

> *Marc sort avec Solange. Cest la fille **avec qui** Pierre est sortie.*
> Marc is going out with Solange. She's the girl **with whom** Peter went out.

Lequel: The Interrogative Pronoun
The relative pronoun *lequel* refers to people or things and could also be used in the preceding sentences: It means **which** or **whom** or **which one**.

> *Marc sort avec Solange. C'est la fille avec **laquelle** Pierre sort.*
> Marc is going out with Solange. She's the girl with whom Pierre goes out. (Or: She's the girl Pierre goes out with.)
> *Mon frère a un serpent **duquel** j'ai peur.*
> My brother has a snake that I am afraid of.
> *Les navires sur **lesquels** sont arrivés les explorateurs n'étaient pas très grands.*
> The ships on which the explorers arrived weren't very big.

Forms of *lequel*:	Singular	Plural
Masculine	*lequel*	*lesquels*
Feminine	*laquelle*	*lesquelles*

As you know, a **pronoun** replaces a noun and must agree in gender and number with that noun.

> *Voici deux pommes. **Laquelle** désires-tu: la pomme verte ou la pomme rouge?*
> Here are two apples. Which one do you want: the green apple or the red apple?
> ***Lequel** des explorateurs était italien?*
> Which one of the explorers was Italian?

These contractions occur with **à:** to which, to whom

Masculine	*auquel*	*auxquels*
Feminine	*à laquelle*	*auxquelles*

De: from/of or about which or whom

Masculine	*duquel*	*desquels*
Feminine	*de laquelle*	*desquelles*

Les pays **auxquels** Brazza est allé sont devenus des colonies
   françaises.
The countries Brazza went to became French colonies.
(The countries to which Brazza went became French colonies.)

La richesse du paysage **duquel** Champlain a parlé a intrigué le roi.
The countryside's richness that Champlain spoke about interested
   the king.
(The countryside's richness about which Champlain spoke interested
   the king.)

La forteresse dans **laquelle** se sont cachés les pionniers était
   primitive.
The fortress the pioneers hid in was primitive.
(The fortress in which the pioneers hid was primitive.)

RAPPEL!

The French usually replace **de qui** (of whom)
and forms of **duquel** (of which) with the word **dont**.

Grammaire
Encore c'est mieux: More Relative Pronouns

Ce que, ce qui, ce dont: **What, that, which, of which**

Ce que, ce qui, and *ce dont* are relative pronouns that don't
have antecedents. When you want to use what, that, or which in
a statement, use these relative pronouns. They follow the same
rules as the pronouns *que, qui,* and *dont*:

> **Ce qui:** subject of the clause, followed by a verb
> **Ce que:** object of the clause, followed by a noun that is the
>   subject of the clause
> **Ce dont:** object of *de*, used in expressions with *de*
>
> Je comprends **ce que** tu veux dire. I understand what you
>   mean.
> **Ce qui** est arrivé était incroyable. What happened was
>   unbelievable.
> **Ce dont** tu as besoin c'est de la patience. What you need
>   is patience.

Où may also be used as a relative pronoun. It is sometimes used instead of the prepositional phrase and *lequel*. It is used to modify a place or a date.

> Saint Malô est la ville **où** Jacques Cartier est né.
> Saint Malo is the town where Jacques Cartier was born.

To avoid the longer:

> Saint Malô est la ville **dans laquelle** Jacques Cartier est né.
>
> L'année **où** je suis né, il a beaucoup neigé.
> The year I was born, it snowed a lot.

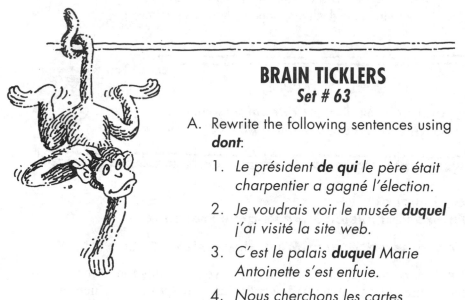

BRAIN TICKLERS
Set # 63

A. Rewrite the following sentences using **dont**:

1. Le président **de qui** le père était charpentier a gagné l'élection.

2. Je voudrais voir le musée **duquel** j'ai visité la site web.

3. C'est le palais **duquel** Marie Antoinette s'est enfuie.

4. Nous cherchons les cartes **desquelles** nous avons besoin.

5. La peinture **de laquelle** la critique écrit est magnifique.

B. Use a form of **lequel** to replace the underlined words, and then combine the sentences:

Ex: Je connais le fleuve Saint Laurent. Québec se trouve <u>sur ce fleuve</u>.
Je connais le fleuve Saint Laurent sur lequel se trouve Québec.

1. Voici une table. Monet a mangé <u>sur cette</u> table.

2. *J'ai visité une île tropicale. Bougainville a atterri près de cette île.*

3. *Nous avons pris des photos. On peut voir un arc-en-ciel dans ces photos.*

4. *Ils ont signé le traité. Dans le traité on a promis de la paix.*

C. Use **ce que, ce qui,** or **ce dont** as necessary:

1. _____ *tu as fait était très apprécié.*

2. _____ *nous avons peur, ce sont les araignées.*

3. _____ *m'intéresse, c'est l'histoire des rois.*

4. *Je ne comprends pas _____ tu dis!*

5. *Comprend-elle _____ se passe?*

(Answers are on page 260.)

Info

Because of the widespread travels of French explorers, there are many towns and cities with French names in the United States. Here are a few French-named places. Try to translate their French meaning.

Eau Clair	*Fond du Lac*	*Baton Rouge*	*Terre Haute*
Detroit	*Presque Isle*	*Lacrosse*	*Boise*
Des Moines	*Vermont*	*Des Plaines*	*Ville Plate*

Even Buffalo comes from the words ***beau fleuve***, beautiful river. Misunderstood and poorly pronounced, it became Buffalo, even though buffalos didn't live there!

Answers:

Clear Water	*Bottom of the Lake*	*Red Stick*	*High Ground*
Narrows	*Almost an Island*	*The Cross*	*Wooded (Place)*
(Of the) Monks	*Green Mountain*	*(Of the) Plains*	*Flat City*

See if you can find other places with French names on a map.

Répète après moi!

qu- in French is <u>always</u> pronounced like **k**: *qui* sounds like **key**. Be careful not to let English interfere with the development of your language skills. Practice pronouncing these words and be sure to make a hard **k** sound:

> quand, questionner, quarantaine, quantité, Quasimodo, quartier, quadrupler, qualifier, tranquille, queue, quête, querelle, quitter
>
> (when, to question, quarantine, quantity, Quasimodo [the Hunchback of Notre Dame], quarter [neighborhood], quadruple, qualify, calm [quiet], tail or line, quest, quarrel, to leave a place)

Vocabulaire: Encore c'est mieux

L'économie	Economy
une augmentation	increase
une banque	bank
un billet	bill of money
la bourse	stock exchange
le bureau de change	currency exchange
une caisse d'épargne	savings bank
une carte bancaire	bank card
une carte de crédit	credit card
un chèque	check
coûter	to cost
DAB (distributeur automatique de billets)	ATM (automatic teller machine)
dépenser	to spend
économiser	to save
en espèces	cash

une hypothèque	mortgage
de l'intérêt	interest
la monnaie	change
payer	to pay
prêter	to lend
profit	profit
retirer de l'argent	withdraw money
taux d'échange	exchange rate
transférer	to transfer

Grammaire
Les pronoms possessifs et démonstratifs
(Possessive and Demonstrative Pronouns)

As you know, pronouns replace nouns, and because French nouns are masculine or feminine, singular or plural, their pronouns will also follow suit.

Possessive pronouns: You know how to say my house, *ma maison*, and his bike, *son vélo*.

To say **mine** and **his,** follow this example, and then look at the chart:

> your house and **mine***: ta maison et* **la mienne**
> my bike and **his***: mon vélo et* **le sien**

Masculine Singular	Masculine Plural	Feminine Singular	Feminine Plural	English
le mien	*les miens*	*la mienne*	*les miennes*	mine
le tien	*les tiens*	*la tienne*	*les tiennes*	yours
le sien	*les siens*	*la sienne*	*les siennes*	his/hers
le nôtre	*les nôtres*	*la nôtre*	*les nôtres*	ours
le vôtre	*les vôtres*	*la vôtre*	*les vôtres*	yours
le leur	*les leurs*	*la leur*	*les leurs*	theirs

Make sure to match the gender and number of the noun you are replacing with the correct form of the possessive pronoun. The following contractions also occur with possessive pronouns:

To / in / at / the $à + le = au / à + les = aux$

From / of / about the $de + le = du / de + les = des$

> *Le prof parlera à ton père et **au mien**.*
> The teacher will talk to your father and to mine.

> *J'ai besoin de mes lunettes. Ont-ils besoins **des leurs**?*
> I need my glasses. Do they need theirs?

Les pronoms démonstratifs (Demonstrative Pronouns)
When you say **this one** or **that one,** you are using demonstrative pronouns.

> *Je veux ce sandwich. Veux-tu **celui**-là?*
> I want this sandwich. Do you want that one?

	Singular	Plural
Masculine	*celui*	*ceux*
Feminine	*celle*	*celles*

By adding *-ci* or *-là,* you can distinguish between **this one** and **that one**.

> *Quelles chaussures sont les tiennes? **Celles**-ci ou **celles**-là?*
> Which shoes are yours? These or those?

> *Quels journaux lis-tu, **ceux-ci** ou **ceux-là**?*
> Which newspapers do you read, these or those?

When used with *de,* the demonstrative pronouns can indicate possession.

> *L'appartement de René et **celui** de Robert sont au sixième étage.*
> René's apartment and Robert's are on the sixth floor.

These forms are also used to express former, *celle-là,* *celui-la* and latter, *celui-ci,* and *celle-ci.*

> *J'ai téléphoné à une banque nationale et à une banque internationale.*
> I called a national bank and an international bank.

> *Celle-ci pouvait échanger mon argent en euros, mais celle-là ne pouvait pas.*
> The latter could change my money into euros, but the former could not.

BRAIN TICKLERS
Set # 64

Possessive and Demonstrative Pronouns

A. Rewrite the following sentences by replacing the underlined words with possessive pronouns.

   1. Ce sont _mes valises_ (f.). Où sont _tes valises?_

   2. Voici _ton appareil-photo_ et _son appareil-photo._

   3. Ils ont _leurs passeports,_ mais nous n'avons pas _nos passeports._

   4. Elle cherche _son portefeuille_ pendant que je cherche _mon portefeuille._

   5. Vous tenez _vos billets_ à la main mais les enfants ne tiennent pas _leurs billets._

B. Respond to the questions using demonstrative pronouns:

   1. C'est ton portefeuille? Non, c'est _____ de mon père.

   2. Ce sont tes chèques de voyage? Non, ce sont _____ de ma mère.

   3. C'est ta valise? Non, c'est _____ de ma sœur.

   4. C'est ton imper? Non, c'est _____ de mon frère.

   5. Quels billets sont les tiens? _____-ci ou _____-là?

(Answers are on page 261.)

C'est curieux!

Francophonie is a term that refers to the speaking of French as part of a national identity or cultural tradition. The term also represents a movement that promotes cultural, scientific, and technical exchanges between the over 274 million people around the world who speak French and share aspects of French culture. The 80 member states and governments of the _OIF,_ or _Organisation internationale de la Francophonie,_ hold annual general meetings in such cities as Dakar (Senégal), Montreux (Suisse), and, in 2016, Antananarivo (Madagascar), with many heads of governments attending.

To learn more you can check the website of the *OIF*, *www.francophonie.org*.

A réfléchir
Haiti

Haiti occupies 37 percent of the Caribbean island shared with the Dominican Republic. The island is the second largest in the Caribbean after Cuba. Originally occupied by the Arawaks and Caribbean peoples, when Christopher Columbus landed in 1492 it became Espaniola. The French part in the east became Saint Domingue, and slaves were imported to work the sugarcane plantations. They spoke Creole, a language that was mixed with their native African language. Early on in its turbulent history the slaves revolted to gain their freedom, lead by Toussaint-Louverture. Over the centuries there were many government changeovers, and the United States took military control in 1915 for a period of time. It is one of the poorest countries in the world with widespread poverty. In January of 2010 more than 300,000 people died in a devastating earthquake, whose effects continue to plague the Haitian population. The capital is Port-au-Prince, and the official languages are French and Creole—98.5 percent of the population is Creole and 1.5 percent is French. The education system has incorporated both languages in the school system, with an emphasis on educating students in Creole since it is their native language. Compare the Creole in the passage that follows with its French translation.

Un exemple de promotion du créole:

Refòm Sistem Edikasyon Ayisyen an Chita Sou Verite Sa Yo

1. Pèp ayisyen an egal ego ak tout lòt pèp. Li fòje yon lang, li tabli yon kilti menm jan ak tout moun.

2. Soti depi li fèt rive jounen jodi a, lang kreyòl ayisyen an kite koridò lang patwa, li pran boulva lang total ki gen fason pa-1 pou kouche-1 sou papye. Nan pwen lang lan rive koulyeya, tout konesans lasyans ak lateknik ka koule dous pase ladan li.

3. Men yon verite moun toupatou rekonèt: Pou fè aprantisaj lekti ak ekriti se nan lang manman timoun nan sa dwe fèt an premye.

4. Pa fouti gen devlopman si pa gen edikasyon. Pa fouti gen devlopman si pa gen inyon tèt ansanm.

5. Gen 2 lang ki sèvi nan peyi a. Men se yon sèl pèp ayisyen an ki genyen. Kidonk, fòk gen yon sòl sistòm ansòyman ki pou sèvi ak tout 2 lang nou yo.

Quelques Vérités Fondamentales Qui Sous-Tendent la Réforme du Système Educatif Haïtien

1. Le peuple haïtien n'est pas inférieur. Il est créateur de langue et de culture, au même titre que tous les autres peuples.

2. Au cours de son évolution, le créole haïtien est passé du stade de patois à celui de langue écrite, standardisée et littéraire. Aujourd'hui, il est capable de véhiculer les connaissances scientifiques et techniques.

3. Il est universellement reconnu que l'apprentissage de la lecture et de l'écriture doit se faire dans la langue maternelle de l'enfant.

4. Pas de développement sans éducation. Pas de développement sans unité.

5. Deux langues: Mais un seul peuple. Donc un seul système d'enseignement, utilisant deux langues.

Vocabulaire

le peuple	people
un créateur	creator
un stade	stadium
un patois	vernacular
véhiculer	to convey
des connaissances	knowledge
reconnu	recognized
un apprentissage	apprenticeship, learning
lecture	reading

Tu sais quoi?

Jacques Roumain was a Haitian writer who lived from 1907 to 1944. He was born in Port-au-Prince to a wealthy family and studied in Europe as a young man. At twenty years old he returned to Haiti and created *La Revue Indigène: Les Arts et La Vie (The Indigenous Review: Arts and Life)*. He was a poet and a novelist who became renowned for his colorful and touching works. In *Gouverneurs de la Rosée (Masters of the Dew)* he wrote of hope in the lives of the poor. His collection of poems is called *Bois Debene (Ebony Wood)*.

Here is an excerpt from *Les Gouverneurs de la Rosée:*

Bienaimé, sur l'étroite galerie fermée par une balustrade ajourée et protégée par l'avancée du toit de chaume, contemplait sa terre, sa bonne terre, ses plantes ruisselantes, ses arbres balancés dans le chant de la pluie et du vent. La récolte serait bonne. Il avait peiné au soleil à longueur de journées. Cette pluie, c'était sa récompense. Il la regardait avec amitié, tomber en filets serrés, il l'écoutait clapoter sur sa dalle de pierre devant la tonnelle. Tant et tant de maïs, tant de pois-Congo, le cochon engraissé: cela ferait une nouvelle vareuse, une chemise et peut-être le poulain bai de voisin Jean-Jacques s'il voulait rabattre sur le prix.

Il avait oublié Délira.

—Chauffez le café, ma femme, dit-il.

Oui, il lui achèterait aussi une robe et un madras.

Il bourra sa courte pipe d'argile. Voilà ce que c'était de vivre en bon ménage avec la terre.

Vocabulaire

une balustrade	railing
ajourée	perforated
un toit du chaume	thatch roof
ruisselantes	dripping
balancés	swaying
la récolte	harvest
peiner	toiled
une récompense	reward
pluie tomber en filets serrés	tight streams of water
clapoter	to splash
la dalle de pierre de devant	front stoop of stone
pois-Congo	local vegetable

engraissé	fattened
la vareuse	blouse
le poulain bai	the bay colt
bourrer	stuff
d'argile	clay
en bon ménage	to get on well together

Une Carte Postale de Haïti

Bonjour!

Ça va? C'est Antoine, le cousin de Sophie. Je t'écris de Haïti où je suis allé faire de l'assistance humanitaire avec mon église. C'est un programme dans lequel nous aidons les habitants à reconstruire des simples habitations. Nous réparons aussi des écoles et d'autres bâtiments endommagés par le tremblement de terre de 2010. Nous avons apporté du matériel scholastique comme des cahiers, des crayons, et des livres. Les gens nous sont accueillants malgré leur situation d'extrême pauvreté. Nous ferons des excursions aux différentes parties de l'île pour voir nous-mêmes la vie des habitants. Nous espérons pouvoir aider autant de gens que possible. Il faut continuer à faire des travaux humanitaires pour aider ces gens à retrouver un niveau de vie normale. Nous sommes en train d'apprendre un peu de créole pour mieux communiquer avec ces gens si necessiteux.

A bientôt, Antoine

Vocabulaire

reconstruire	rebuild
un tremblement de terre	earthquake
accueillants	welcoming
malgré	in spite of
la pauvreté	poverty
necessiteux	needy

Proverbe: Didier dit

Après la pluie, le beau temps.
Every cloud has a silver lining.
(Literally: After the rain, good weather.)

BRAIN TICKLERS
Set # 65

Haïti et Vocabulaire

A. Lisez et écrivez les verbes qui sont définis:

1. *travailler très dur:* _____

2. *communiquer:* _____

3. *mettre beaucoup de quelque chose dans un endroit limité:* _____

4. *le bruit d'eau:* _____

B. Répondez aux questions sur le système éducatif de Haïti:

1. *Quel était le premier stade de la langue Créole?*

2. *Comment est-ce que cela a changé?*

3. *En quelle langue est-ce qu'un enfant doit commencer à lire et à écrire?*

4. *Quels deux éléments sont nécessaires pour le développement?*

(Answers are on page 261.)

Amis/Faux Amis

You probably recognized many *amis* in the vocabulary; *la banque, armée, ambassadeur,* and *président* are a few examples. But note the following *faux amis*:

> Le frontière means the border, not the Wild West.
> La monnaie refers to change or coins.

BRAIN TICKLERS — THE ANSWERS

Set # 62, page 244

A.

1. *président*
2. *voter*
3. *armée*
4. *abolir*
5. *maintenir*

B.

1. *qui*
2. *qu'*
3. *qui*
4. *qui*
5. *que*

Set # 63, page 248

A.

1. *Le président dont le père était charpentier a gagné l'élection.*
2. *Je voudrais voir le musée dont j'ai visité la site web.*
3. *C'est le palais dont Marie Antoinette s'est enfuie.*
4. *Nous cherchons les cartes dont nous avons besoin.*
5. *La peinture dont la critique écrit est magnifique.*

B.

1. *Voici une table sur laquelle Monet a mangé.*
2. *J'ai visité une île tropicale près de laquelle Bougainville a atterri.*
3. *Nous avons pris des photos dans lesquelles on peut voir un arc-en-ciel.*
4. *Ils ont signé le traité dans lequel on a promis de la paix.*

C.

1. *Ce que*
2. *Ce dont*
3. *Ce qui*
4. *ce que*
5. *ce qui*

Set # 64, page 253

A.

1. *Ce sont les miennes. Où sont les tiennes?*
2. *Voici le tien et le sien.*
3. *Ils ont les leurs, mais nous n'avons pas les nôtres.*
4. *Elle cherche le sien pendant que je cherche le mien.*
5. *Vous tenez les vôtres à la main mais les enfants ne tiennent pas les leurs.*

B.

1. *celui*
2. *ceux*
3. *celle*
4. *celui*
5. *Ceux, ceux*

Set # 65, page 259

A.

1. *peiner*
2. *véhiculer*
3. *bourrer*
4. *clapoter*

B.

1. *C'était d'abord un patois.*
2. *Maintenant on peut l'utiliser pour communiquer des idées scientifiques ou techniques.*
3. *Un enfant doit commencer son éducation dans sa langue maternelle (la créole ici).*
4. *L'éducation et l'unité sont nécessaires.*

J'apprécie l'histoire de mon pays

I LOVE MY COUNTRY'S HISTORY

Salut! C'est Sophie.

C'est la dernière fois que je t'écris, et je vais parler de l'histoire de France. Le passé préhistorique me fascine. Les grottes de Lascaux en Dordogne ont les peintures préhistoriques les plus célèbres du monde. Les couleurs et formes des animaux (surtout les chevaux) sont magnifiques. En Bretagne il y a des menhirs et des dolmens dont on ne sait pas exactement l'origine. Ceux-là sont des grands blocs de pierre alignés dans des champs; ceux-ci sont des blocs en forme de table qui servaient peut-être de tombeaux. Les Romains ont conquis la Gaule en 54 avant notre ère. Les Gaulois étaient un peuple qui savait cultiver la terre et l'esprit. Vercingétorix, un chef gaulois, est considéré comme le premier héros français. Il a organisé les Gaulois contre les Romains avant d'être capturé. La civilisation des Gaulois est illustrée dans la bande dessinée Astérix. *Quelques-uns des rois les plus célèbres sont Charlemagne, qui était empereur en 800; Guillaume le Conquérant, qui a conquis l'Angleterre en 1066; et Louis XIV, qu'on appelait le Roi Soleil et qui a fait construire Versailles au dix-septième siècle. Napoléon a régné après la Révolution française (1789), et il a vendu la Louisiane aux Etats-Unis en 1803. Il y a eu quatre républiques avant*  *notre époque. La cinquième République avait comme premier président le général Charles de Gaulle en 1958 au 1969. La France est une république démocratique et sociale. Tous les citoyens français de dix-huit ans ont le droit de voter. Les présidents sont élus pour sept ans. Il y a un premier ministre et le Conseil des ministres pour gouverner et superviser les nouvelles lois. Ils sont responsables devant L'Assemblée nationale et le Sénat. La dévise de la France c'est « Liberté, Égalité, Fraternité. » J'espère que tu feras des recherches plus profondes pour apprendre plus sur notre histoire.*

Au revoir, Sophie

Vocabulaire

L'histoire	History
alignés	aligned
un/une citoyen (citoyenne)	citizen
conquis (from conquérir)	to conquer
un couronnement	coronation
une dévise	motto
un dolmen	table-shaped rock monument
le droit	the right
l'égalité	equality
des élections (f.)	elections
un empereur	emperor
la fraternité	fraternity, brotherhood
une grotte	cave
une loi	law
la liberté	liberty
un menhir	free-standing rock monument
un ministre	minister (of government)
une pierre	rock
un siècle	century
le suffrage	the right to vote
un tombeau	tomb

Des verbes l'histoire	History
adopter	to adopt
élire	to elect
régner	to rule
révolter	to revolt
taxer	to tax
voter	to vote

BRAIN TICKLERS
Set # 66

Match the vocabulary words:

1. ____ *un couronnement*   a. century
2. ____ *le suffrage*   b. motto
3. ____ *une dévise*   c. citizen
4. ____ *un siècle*   d. tomb
5. ____ *un tombeau*   e. vote
6. ____ *un citoyen*   f. coronation

(Answers are on page 280.)

Grammaire
Le passé simple (The Literary Past Tense)

When you read literature or history, you will encounter the
***passé simple*,** or **literary past tense**. It is not used for
conversation like the passé composé, but it has the same
meaning, a completed event in the past. The imperfect is
used with the passé simple to describe incomplete actions or
descriptions. As its name suggests, it is a single or simple tense.
You should be able to recognize easily most verbs as you read.

> *La reine **parla** sérieusement au roi.*
> The queen spoke seriously to the king.

Read the following exerpt from *Le Petit Prince* (*The Little Prince*)
by Antoine de Saint-Exupéry to see how the passé simple is used:

> *Chapitre 2: Le petit prince arrivé au Désert Sahara surprend
> le narrateur qui est un aviateur tombé en panne, avec une
> requête étonnant:*
> *—Chez moi c'est tout petit. J'ai besoin d'un mouton. Dessine-
> moi un mouton.*
> *Alors j'ai dessiné: (dessin d'un mouton qui a l'air malade)*
> *—Non! Celui-là est déjà très malade. Fais-en un autre.*
> *Je **dessinai**: (dessin d'un bélier [ram])*
> *Mon ami **sourit** gentiment, avec indulgence:*

—*Tu vois bien . . . ce n'est pas
un mouton, c'est un bélier. Il a
des cornes . . .*
*Je **refis** donc encore mon
dessin (dessin d'un vieux mouton)
Mais il **fut** refusé, comme les précédents:*
    —*Celui-là est trop vieux. Je veux un mouton qui vive
longtemps.*
*Alors, faute de patience, comme j'avais hâte de commencer
le démontage de mon moteur, je **griffonnai** ce dessin-ci.
(dessin d'une boite avec trois trous sur le côté)
Et je **lançai**:*
    —*Ça c'est la caisse. Le mouton que tu veux est dedans.*
*Mais je **fus** bien surpris de voir s'illuminer le visage de mon
jeune juge:*
    —*C'est tout à fait comme ça que je le voulais!*

Vocabulaire

en panne	broken down
un mouton	sheep
dessiner	to draw
gentiment	kindly
refis (refaire)	to redo
fut (être)	was (verb: to be)
avoir hâte de	to be in a hurry to
griffonnai (griffonner)	to scratch out; draw quickly
lançai (lancer)	to toss out
la caisse	case
dedans	inside
s'illuminer	to light up

Notice that the actions were written in the passé simple.
To form the passé simple:

> **-*er* verbs: Drop the -*er* and add -*ai*, -*as*, -*a*,
> -*âmes*, -*âtes*, -*èrent*:**

Je parlai   Nous parlâmes
Tu parlas   Vous parlâtes
Il/elle parla   Ils/elles parlèrent

-ir and -re verbs: Drop the -ir/-re and add -is, -is, -it, -îmes, -îtes, -irent:

Je finis   Nous finîmes   Je vendis   Nous vendîmes
Tu finis   Vous finîtes   Tu vendis   Vous vendîtes
Il/elle finit   Ils/elles finirent Il/elle vendit   Ils/elles vendirent

BRAIN TICKLERS
Set # 67

A. Questions sur *Le Petit Prince.* Répondez en français.

1. *Où est-ce que cette scène a lieu?*

2. *De quoi est-ce que le Petit Prince a besoin?*

3. *Qu'est-ce que le narrateur fait?*

4. *Qu'est-ce que le Petit Prince pense du deuxième mouton?*

5. *Quel mouton est-ce que le Petit Prince préfère?*

B. Write these verbs in the passé simple:

1. *Louis XIV* _____ *la France au dix-septième siècle. (regner)*

2. *Vercingétorix* _____ *les Gaulois contre les romains. (organiser)*

3. *Les romains* _____ *la Gaule. (envahir)*

4. *Napoléon* _____ *la Louisiane aux Américains en 1803. (vendre)*

5. *Les révolutionnaires* _____ *la liberté, l'égalité, et le fraternité. (demander)*

(Answers are on page 280.)

Grammaire
Le passé simple des verbes irréguliers
(Irregular Verbs in the Past Simple Tense)

Most irregular verbs are recognizable if you know their past participles. **Past participles that end with u, add -s, -s, -t, -ûmes, -ûtes, -ûrent.**

> **Pouvoir:** *je pus, tu pus, il put, nous pûmes, vous pûtes, ils purent*

Infinitive	Past Participle	Passé Simple	English
avoir	*eu*	*il eut*	he had
boire	*bu*	*il but*	he drank
courir	*couru*	*il courut*	he ran
lire	*lu*	*il lut*	he read
recevoir	*reçu*	*il reçut*	he received
savoir	*su*	*il sut*	he knew
vivre	*vécu*	*il vécut*	he lived
vouloir	*voulu*	*il voulut*	he wanted

Past participles that end with i or is/it have the same endings: *-is, -is, -it, -îmes, -îtes, -îrent.*

> **Dormir:** *je dormis, tu dormis, il dormit, nous dormîmes, vous dormîtes, ils dormirent*

> **Conquérir:** *je conquis, tu conquis, il conquit, nous conquîmes, vous conquîtes, ils conquirent*

Infinitive	Past Participle	Passé Simple	English
dire	*dit*	*il dit*	he said
mettre	*mis*	*il mit*	he put on or placed
partir	*parti*	*il partit*	he left
prendre	*pris*	*il prit*	he took
sentir	*senti*	*il sentit*	he smelled
sortir	*sorti*	*il sortit*	he went out
sourire	*souri*	*il sourit*	he smiled
suivre	*suivi*	*il suivit*	he followed

Passé simple verbs with irregular patterns: Some verbs in the passé simple do not use past participles as stems. Learn to recognize the following irregular verbs: the endings are *-s, -s, -t, -mes, -tes, -rent.*

Infinitive	Passé Simple	English	Past Participle
battre	*il battit*	he beat	*battu*
conduire	*il conduisit*	he drove	*conduit*
couvrir	*il couvrit*	he covered	*couvert*
être	*il fut*	he was	*été*
détruire	*il détruisit*	he destroyed	*détruit*
faire	*il fit*	he did	*fait*
mourir	*il mourut*	he died	*mort*
naître	*il naquit*	he was born	*né*
offrir	*il offrit*	he offered	*offert*
peindre	*il peignit*	he painted	*peint*
vaincre	*il vainquit*	he vanquished	*vaincu*
venir	*il vint*	he came	*venu*
voir	*il vit*	he saw	*vu*

BRAIN TICKLERS
Set # 68

A. Rewrite the passé simple verbs into the passé composé:

1. *Nous **bûmes** l'eau de la source.*

2. *Les habitants de Lascaux **peignirent** des beaux chevaux.*

3. *Le peuple de Paris **détruisit** la Bastille.*

4. *Napoléon **mourut** sur l'Ile de Sainte-Hélène.*

5. *Samuel de Champlain **découvrit** Québec.*

B. Give the infinitive of the verb for these passé simple verbs:

1. *nous fîmes*
2. *ils eurent*
3. *elle naquit*
4. *vous vîtes*
5. *elles voulurent*
6. *il fut*

(Answers are on page 281.)

Répète après moi!

The sound *gne* is a common sound in French. It is similar to the g in *pang*, but stretch it out a little longer by keeping the back of your tongue against your palate. Say the following words:

> *campagne, montagne, Allemagne, Champagne, Bretagne, Bourgogne, Auvergne*
> (country, mountain, Germany, Champagne, Brittany, Burgundy, Auvergne)
> *craigner, grogner, aligner, souligner, renseigner, régner, baigner, accompagner*
> (to fear, to growl, to align, to underline, to give information, to rule, to bathe, to accompany)

Info

France's economy is ranked among the top ten worldwide. It has the lowest poverty rate of the large economic powers. France also has some of the world's best public and social services. France leads Europe in exports and has a very strong agricultural tradition. France also has major construction, chemical, pharmaceutical, fashion, perfume, automobile, and communications industries. Many former French colonies still have strong economic ties to France. Francophone businessmen and leaders are often educated in Paris. France has played a vital role in the development of humanitarian action and international law concerning humanitarian aid. The international medical humanitarian organization Médecins Sans Frontières/Doctors Without Borders was created by doctors and journalists in France in 1971; MSF won the Nobel Peace Prize in 1999 and in 2015 won the Lasker Award for its bold leadership and response to the Ebola outbreak in Africa. France also contributes substantially to humanitarian programs of the United Nations such as UNICEF and World Food Programme.

Vocabulaire

la Presse/les Actualités	The Press/The News
à la une	the front page
un article	article
le courrier	letters/mail
le courrier du cœur	advice column
le critique	critic
un/une éditeur/éditrice	publisher
imprimer	to print
un journal	newspaper
un/une journaliste	journalist
des petites annonces (f.)	classified ads
la presse écrite	the written press
une publicité	advertisement
un quotidien	daily
un rédacteur	editor
une rubrique	column/section

L'Ordinateur	The Computer
une cartouche d'encre	ink cartridge
un clavier	keyboard
une clé USB	flashdrive
cliquer	to click
couper-coller	cut and paste
un courrier électronique	email
un écran	screen
mot de passe	password
un navigateur	web browser

273

un nom de l'utilisateur	user name
un pare-feu	firewall
une photo-numérique	digital photo
un pourriel	spam
un raccourci	shortcut
tchatter	to chat
télécharger	download
tweeter	to tweet

http://jeanboulanger.com/lexique/Lexique_Informatique.pdf

Grammaire
Les adverbes (Adverbs)

Adverbs in French are placed directly after the verb:

> *Il parle souvent de son pays.* He often speaks of his country.
> *Le journaliste écrit vite son article sur son ordinateur.* The journalist writes his article quickly on his computer.

Common Irregular Adverbs

bas	low	*peu*	little
bien	well	*rarement*	rarely
mal	poorly	*souvent*	often
moins	less	*vite*	quickly

Most **adverbs** are formed by adding **-ment** on the end of the feminine form of adjectives: **-ment** is translated into English as **-ly**.

Feminine Adjective	Adverb	English
extrême	*extrêmement*	extremely
fausse	*faussement*	falsely
finale	*finalement*	finally
folle	*follement*	crazily
heureuse	*heureusement*	fortunately
lente	*lentement*	slowly
naturelle	*naturellement*	naturally
sérieuse	*sérieusement*	seriously

If the masculine form of the adjective ends in a vowel, then use it as the base:

Masculine Adjective	Adverb	English
vrai	*vraiment*	really
sincère	*sincèrement*	sincerely
rapide	*rapidement*	rapidly
facile	*facilement*	easily
poli	*poliment*	politely
absolu	*absolument*	absolutely

If the French adjective ends in **ant** or **ent**, then the endings are **-amment** and **-emment**.

Masculine Adjective	Adverb	English
constant	*constamment*	constantly
courant	*couramment*	fluently
evident	*évidemment*	evidently
intelligent	*intelligemment*	intelligently
brillant	*brillamment*	brilliantly
patient	*patiemment*	patiently
prudent	*prudemment*	carefully

Some adverbs add *–ément* to the following adjectives:

Feminine Adjective	Adverb	English
confuse	*confusément*	confusingly
énorme	*énormément*	enormously
obscure	*obscurément*	obscurely
précise	*précisément*	precisely
profonde	*profondément*	profoundly

To compare adverbs, use *plus*, *moins*, and *aussi* just like adjective comparisons, but of course agreement is not an issue.

> *Le reporter parle français **plus couramment** que l'éditeur.*
> The reporter speaks French more fluently than the publisher.
> *Je lis les bandes dessinées **aussi souvent** que l'horoscope.*
> I read the comics as often as I read the horoscope.

The superlative uses *le plus* and *le moins*.

> *Le critique parle **le plus sérieusement** de la pièce.*
> The critic speaks the most seriously about the play.

*Les enfants attendent **le moins impatiemment**.*
The children wait the most impatiently.

When using *bien* (well), the comparative form for "better" is *mieux*, and superlative words for "the best" are *le mieux*:

*Thomas chante **bien**.* Thomas sings well.
*Marie-France chante **mieux** que lui.* Marie-France sings better than he does.
*Chantal chante **le mieux** de tous.* Chantal sings the best of all.

When using *mal* ("badly") you may say the comparative form "worse" two ways: *plus mal* or *pis*. The superlative form "the worst" is *le plus mal* or *le pis*.

*Paul danse **pis** que moi, mais Marie danse **le pis** de tous.*
*Paul danse **plus mal** que moi, mais Marie danse **le plus mal** de tous.*
Paul dances worse than I do, but Marie dances the worst of all.

BRAIN TICKLERS
Set # 69

A. Change these adjectives into adverbs:
  1. *joli*
  2. *tranquille*
  3. *heureux*
  4. *constant*
  5. *énorme*

B. Translate the following sentences:
  1. M. LeBlanc speaks English more fluently than Mme LeBlanc.
  2. We study most seriously before a test.
  3. The journalist writes less often about sports.
  4. My sister cooks the worst in my family.
  5. I play cards the best.

(Answers are on page 281.)

A réfléchir
Louisiana and New England: Francophone Regions in the United States

From 1765 to 1785 the English deported thousands of Acadians from Acadia, the eastern region of Canada today known as Nova Scotia (*La Nouvelle Ecosse*). Families were separated and shipped off to Louisiana. The approximately 3,000 Acadians who went to Louisiana became known as Cajuns, and after many years of struggle they created their own culture in Louisiana. The CODOFIL, the Council for the Development of French in Louisiana, was founded in 1968. Its purpose is to preserve, develop, and utilize the French language for the cultural, economic, and touristic benefit of the state. It is estimated that 250,000 people living in Louisiana are of French origin. See *www.codofil.org* to read about CODOFIL in French, English, or Creole.

A large portion of the population of New England also speaks French because approximately 900,000 Canadians emigrated there between the 1840s and the 1930s. These Franco-Americans are proud of their heritage, and writers and singers express their French heritage.

Tu sais quoi?

Zachary Richard was born in Scott, Louisiana, and grew up speaking Creole, French, and English. Zachary started singing when he was eight years old, and later as a rock and roll fan, he began to write about his Cajun experience with depth and poetry. Not only does he write about his French cultural heritage, but he is also active in defending environmental issues. He has lived in the Bayou, New York, and Quebec over the years and enjoys writing poems too. He has written a documentary, *Contre vents, contre marées (Against the Tide)*, which is a film about the Cajun people from their French origins to the present day. He continues to publish poetry and music, maintain pages on Facebook, and write a blog that promotes the culture of Cajuns and French Canadians. You may learn more about him by visiting his official website, *www.zacharyrichard.com*.

Ma Louisianne

Oublie voir pas qu'on est Cadien,
Mes chers garçons et mes chères petites filles.
On était en Louisianne avant les Américains,
On sera ici quand ils seront partis.
Ton papa et ta mama étaient chassés de l'Acadie,
Pour le grand crime d'être Cadien.
Mais ils ont trouvé un beau pays,
Merci, Bon Dieu, pour la Louisianne.
Refrain:
La Louisianne, ma Louisianne
Si belle au printemps,
Si chaude en été,
Si fraîche en automne,
Si trempe en hiver,
Mais, mais moi je suis fier d'être Cadien
Oublie voir pas mes chers enfants,
Les manières du vieux temps passé.
Le ciel et la terre ont beaucoup à nous montrer,
Ecoute les paroles des vieux Cadiens.

—Zachary Richard, *Les Editions du Marais Bouleu*

Vocabulaire

oublie voir pas	don't forget to see
chassés	chased
doux/douce	sweet
fraîche	cool (f.)
trempe	damp
fier	proud
paroles	lyrics, words

Une Carte Postale de la Nouvelle Orléans

Salut Sophie!

Je t'écris de la Nouvelle Orléans. C'est une vieille ville où on peut goûter des spécialités cajuns comme la jambalaya (un plat de poulet, riz, crevettes, du saucisson, des légumes comme des oignons, et des poivrons, des tomates, et, bien sûr, des épices piquantes). On mange aussi des plats avec des écrevisses (crawfish). Il y a des desserts magnifiques aussi. Si tu aimes la musique il faut venir visiter cette ville animée: le zydéco (musique cajun), le jazz, le blues, le funk, le Gospel, le reggae, le swing, et encore plus. Le français qu'on parle ici est un peu différent, mais quand on s'y habitue c'est facile. Nous avons visité les bayous en bateau pour voir des alligators, les marais (swamps) de cyprès, et même le Mississippi. Notre guide était un vrai trappeur cajun qui nous a parlé des plantes médicinales aussi bien que l'histoire des premiers Acadiens ou cajuns à arriver. Ce soir nous allons nous promener dans le quartier français et comme on dit nous allons "Laisser le bon temps rouler" (Let the good times roll).

Ton ami, Serge

BRAIN TICKLERS
Set # 70

Complete the following sentences in French:

1. *Un chanteur célèbre de musique zydeco ou cajun s'appelle* _____
   _____.

2. *Le bayou est un* _____
   _____ *de cyprès.*

3. *En Louisiane il fait* _____
   en automne selon la chanson.

4. La Nouvelle Ecosse était appelé _____.

5. Un repas de poulet, saucisson, riz, et tomates est

_____.

(Answers are on page 281.)

Amis/Faux Amis

Liberté, taxer, voter, constant, tranquille are a few examples of the many *amis* you find in this chapter. Here are some *faux amis* you may have noticed:

> *Ministre* refers to a minister of government, much like a cabinet officer in the United States.
> *Un éditeur* is a publisher; the French word for "editor" is *rédacteur/rédactrice*.
> *Un journal* is a newspaper.
> *Un meeting* is a political rally.

BRAIN TICKLERS—THE ANSWERS

Set # 66, page 267

1. f
2. e
3. b

4. a
5. d
6. c

4. *Le Petit Prince pense que le deuxième mouton ressemble à un bélier.*

5. *Le Petit Prince préfèrè le mouton qui est dans la caisse.*

Set # 67, page 269

A.
1. *La scéne a lieu au Désert Sahara.*
2. *Le Petit Prince a besoin d'un mouton.*
3. *Le narrateur dessine trois moutons.*

B.
1. *régna*
2. *organisa*
3. *envahirent*
4. *vendit*
5. *demandèrent*

Set # 68, page 271

A.
1. *Nous avons bu . . .*
2. *Les habitants de Lascaux ont peint . . .*
3. *Le peuple de Paris ont détruit . . .*
4. *Napoléon est mort . . .*
5. *Samuel de Champlain a découvert . . .*

B.
1. *faire*
2. *avoir*
3. *naître*
4. *voir*
5. *vouloir*
6. *être*

Set # 69, page 276

A.
1. *joliment*
2. *tranquillement*
3. *heureusement*
4. *constamment*
5. *énormément*

B.
1. *M LeBlanc parle anglais plus couramment que Mme LeBlanc.*
2. *Nous étudions le plus sérieusement avant un examen.*
3. *Le journaliste écrit moins souvent des sports.*
4. *Ma sœur fait la cuisine le pis/le plus mal de la famille.*
5. *Je joue aux cartes le mieux.*

Set # 70, page 279

1. *Zachary Richard*
2. *marais*
3. *doux*
4. *Acadie*
5. *jambalaya*

APPENDIX

Regular verb conjugations: The big three

	Aimer -er			Grandir -ir			Rendre -re		
le participe présent present participle	aimant liking			grandissant growing			rendant giving back		
le présent present tense	j'aime tu aimes il* aime	nous aimons vous aimez ils* aiment		je grandis tu grandis il grandit	nous grandissons vous grandissez ils grandissent		je rends tu rends il rend	nous rendons vous rendez il rendent	
l'imperatif the imperative	aime aimons aimez			grandis grandissons grandissez			rends rendons rendez		
l'imparfait imperfect tense	j'aimais tu aimais il aimait	nous aimions vous aimiez ils aimaient		je grandissais tu grandissais il grandissait	nous grandissions vous grandissiez ils grandissaient		je rendais tu rendais il rendait	nous rendions vous rendiez ils rendaient	
le futur future tense	j'aimerai tu aimeras il aimera	nous aimerons vous aimerez ils aimeront		je grandirai tu grandiras il grandira	nous grandirons vous grandirez ils grandiront		je rendrai tu rendras il rendra	nous rendrons vous rendrez ils rendront	
le conditionnel conditional tense	j'aimerais tu aimerais il aimerait	nous aimerions vous aimeriez ils aimeraient		je grandirais tu grandirais il grandirait	nous grandirions vous grandiriez ils grandiraient		je rendrais tu rendrais il rendrait	nous rendrions vous rendriez ils rendraient	

* il and elle share the same forms just as ils and elles do.

	aimer	grandir	rendre
le passé simple simple past tense	j'aimai tu aimas il aima / nous aimâmes vous aimâtes ils aimèrent	je grandis tu grandis il grandit / nous grandîmes vous grandîtes ils grandirent	je rendis tu rendis il rendit / nous rendîmes vous rendîtes ils rendirent
le subjonctif subjunctive mood	j'aime tu aimes il aime / nous aimions vous aimiez ils aiment	je grandisse tu grandisses il grandisse / nous grandissions vous grandissiez ils grandissent	je rende tu rendes il rende / nous rendions vous rendiez ils rendent

Compound tenses follow the forms of avoir or être combined with the corresponding past participle.

	aimer	grandir	rendre
le passé composé past tense	j'ai aimé (present of avoir)	j'ai grandi	j'ai rendu
le plus que parfait pluperfect	j'avais aimé (imperfect of avoir)	j'avais grandi	j'avais rendu
le conditionnel passé past conditional	j'aurais aimé (conditional of avoir)	j'aurais grandi	j'aurais rendu
le futur antérieur the future perfect	j'aurai aimé (future of avoir)	j'aurai grandi	j'aurai rendu
le passé du subjonctif past subjunctive	j'aie aimé (present subjunctive of avoir)	j'aie grandi	j'aie rendu

Irregular verb chart: The big four

	Avoir	Aller	Être	Faire
le participe présent present participle	ayant having	allant going	étant being	faisant doing, making
le présent present tense	j'ai nous avons tu as vous avez il* a ils* ont	je vais nous allons tu vas vous allez il va ils vont	je suis nous sommes tu es vous êtes il est ils sont	je fais nous faisons tu fais vous faites il fait ils font
l'imperatif the imperative	aie ayons ayez	va allons allez	sois soyons soyez	fais faisons faites
l'imparfait imperfect tense	j'avais nous avions tu avais vous aviez il avait ils avaient	j'allais nous allions tu allais vous alliez il allait ils allaient	j'étais nous étions tu étais vous étiez il était ils étaient	je faisais nous faisions tu faisais vous faisiez il faisait ils faisaient
le futur future tense	j'aurai nous aurons tu auras vous aurez il aura ils auront	j'irai nous irons tu iras vous irez il ira ils iront	je serai nous serons tu seras vous serez il sera ils seront	je ferai nous ferons tu feras vous ferez il fera ils feront
le conditionnel conditional tense	j'aurais nous aurions tu aurais vous auriez il aurait ils auraient	j'irais nous irions tu irais vous iriez il irait ils iraient	je serais nous serions tu serais vous seriez il serait ils seraient	je ferais nous ferions tu ferais vous feriez il ferait ils feraient

* il and elle share the same forms just as ils and elles do.

	avoir	aller	être	faire
le passé simple / simple past tense	j'eus, tu eus, il eut, nous eûmes, vous eûtes, ils eurent	j'allai, tu allas, il alla, nous allâmes, vous allâtes, ils allèrent	je fus, tu fus, il fut, nous fûmes, vous fûtes, ils furent	je fis, tu fis, il fit, nous fîmes, vous fîtes, ils firent
le subjonctif / subjunctive mood	j'aie, tu aies, il ait, nous ayons, vous ayez, ils aient	j'aille, tu ailles, il aille, nous allions, vous alliez, ils aillent	je sois, tu sois, il soit, nous soyons, vous soyez, ils soient	je fasse, tu fasses, il fasse, nous fassions, vous fassiez, ils fassent

Compound tenses follow the forms of avoir or être above combined with the corresponding past participle.

	avoir	être	faire
le passé composé / past tense	j'ai eu (present of avoir)	je suis allé (e) (present tense of être)	j'ai fait
le plus que parfait / pluperfect	j'avais eu (imperfect of avoir)	j'étais allé(e) (imperfect of être)	j'avais fait
le conditionnel passé / past conditional	j'aurais eu (conditional of avoir)	je serais allé(e) (conditional of être)	j'aurais fait
le futur antérieur / the future perfect	j'aurai eu (future of avoir)	je serais allé(e) (future of être)	j'aurai fait
le passé du subjonctif / past subjunctive	j'aie eu (present subjunctive of avoir)	je sois allé(e) (present subjunctive of être)	j'aie fait

Irregular verb chart: other irregular verbs, part one

	Boire	Devoir	Pouvoir	Vouloir
le participe présent present participle	buvant drinking	devant owing, having to	pouvant being able	voulant wanting
le présent present tense	je bois · nous buvons tu bois · vous buvez il* boit · ils* boivent	je dois · nous devons tu dois · vous devez il doit · ils doivent	je peux · nous pouvons tu peux · vous pouvez il peut · ils peuvent	je veux · nous voulons tu veux · vous voulez il veut · ils veulent
l'impératif the imperative	bois buvons buvez	dois devons devez		veuille (veux) veuillons (voulons) veuillez (voulez)
l'imparfait imperfect tense	je buvais · nous buvions tu buvais · vous buviez il buvait · ils buvaient	je devais · nous devions tu devais · vous deviez il devait · ils devaient	je pouvais · nous pouvions tu pouvais · vous pouviez il pouvait · ils pouvaient	je voulais · nous voulions tu voulais · vous vouliez il voulait · ils voulaient
le futur future tense	je boirai · nous boirons tu boiras · vous boirez il boira · ils boiront	je devrai · nous devrons tu devras · vous devrez il devra · ils devront	je pourrai · nous pourrons tu pourras · vous pourrez il pourra · ils pourront	je voudrai · nous voudrons tu voudras · vous voudrez il voudra · ils voudront
le conditionnel conditional tense	je boirais · nous boirions tu boirais · vous boiriez il boirait · ils boiraient	je devrais · nous devrions tu devrais · vous devriez il devrait · ils devraient	je pourrais · nous pourrions tu pourrais · vous pourriez il pourrait · ils pourraient	je voudrais · nous voudrions tu voudrais · vous voudriez il voudrait · ils voudraient

* il and elle share the same forms just as ils and elles do.

le passé simple simple past tense	je bus / nous bûmes tu bus / vous bûtes il but / ils burent	je dus / nous dûmes tu dus / vous dûtes il dut / ils durent	je pus / nous pûmes tu pus / vous pûtes il put / ils purent	je voulus / nous voulûmes tu voulus / vous voulûtes il voulut / ils voulurent
le subjonctif subjunctive mood	je boive / nous buvions tu boives / vous buviez il boive / ils boivent	je doive / nous devions tu doives / vous deviez il doive / ils doivent	je puisse / nous puissions tu puisses / vous puissiez il puisse / ils puissent	je veuille / nous voulions tu veuilles / vous vouliez il veuille / ils veuillent

Compound tenses use avoir or être as helping verbs combined with the corresponding past participle.

le passé composé past tense	j'ai bu (present of avoir)	j'ai dû	j'ai pu	j'ai voulu
le plus que parfait pluperfect	j'avais bu (imperfect of avoir)	j'avais dû	j'avais pu	j'avais voulu
le conditionnel passé past conditional	j'aurais bu (conditional of avoir)	j'aurais dû	j'aurais pu	j'aurais voulu
le futur antérieur the future perfect	j'aurai bu (future of avoir)	j'aurai dû	j'aurai pu	j'aurai voulu
le passé du subjonctif past subjunctive	j'aie bu (present subjunctive of avoir)	j'aie dû	j'aie pu	j'aie voulu

Irregular verb chart: other irregular verbs, part two

	Dire	Écrire	Lire	Prendre
le participe présent present participle	disant saying	écrivant writing	lisant reading	prenant taking
le présent present tense	je dis / tu dis / il* dit nous disons / vous dites / ils* disent	j'écris / tu écris / il écrit nous écrivons / vous écrivez / ils écrivent	je lis / tu lis / il lit nous lisons / vous lisez / ils lisent	je prends / tu prends / il prend nous prenons / vous prenez / ils prennent
l'impératif the imperative	dis / disons / dites	écris / écrivons / écrivez	lis / lisons / lisez	prends / prenons / prenez
l'imparfait imperfect tense	je disais / tu disais / il disait nous disions / vous disiez / ils disaient	j'écrivais / tu écrivais / il écrivait nous écrivions / vous écriviez / ils écrivaient	je lisais / tu lisais / il lisait nous lisions / vous lisiez / ils lisaient	je prenais / tu prenais / il prenait nous prenions / vous preniez / ils prenaient
le futur future tense	je dirai / tu diras / il dira nous dirons / vous direz / ils diront	j'écrirai / tu écriras / il écrira nous écrirons / vous écrirez / ils écriront	je lirai / tu liras / il lira nous lirons / vous lirez / ils liront	je prendrai / tu prendras / il prendra nous prendrons / vous prendrez / ils prendront
le conditionnel conditional tense	je dirais / tu dirais / il dirait nous dirions / vous diriez / ils diraient	j'écrirais / tu écrirais / il écrirait nous écririons / vous écririez / ils écriraient	je lirais / tu lirais / il lirait nous lirions / vous liriez / ils liraient	je prendrais / tu prendrais / il prendrait nous prendrions / vous prendriez / ils prendraient

* il and elle share the same forms just as ils and elles do.

	dire	écrire	lire	prendre
le passé simple simple past tense	je dis nous dîmes tu dis vous dîtes il dit ils dirent	j'écrivis nous écrivîmes tu écrivis vous écrivîtes il écrit ils écrivirent	je lus nous lûmes tu lus vous lûtes il lut ils lurent	je pris nous prîmes tu pris vous prîtes il prit ils prirent
le subjonctif subjunctive mood	je dise nous disions tu dises vous disiez il dise ils disent	j'écrive nous écrivions tu écrives vous écriviez il écrive ils écrivent	je lise nous lisions tu lises vous lisiez il lise ils lisent	je prenne nous prenions tu prennes vous preniez il prenne ils prennent

Compound tenses use *avoir* or *être* as helping verbs combined with the corresponding past participle.

le passé composé past tense	j'ai dit (present of avoir)	j'ai écrit	j'ai lu	j'ai pris
le plus que parfait pluperfect	j'avais dit (imperfect of avoir)	j'avais écrit	j'avais lu	j'avais pris
le conditionnel passé past conditional	j'aurais dit (conditional of avoir)	j'aurais écrit	j'aurais lu	j'aurais pris
le futur antérieur the future perfect	j'aurai dit (future of avoir)	j'aurai écrit	j'aurai lu	j'aurai pris
le passé du subjonctif past subjunctive	j'aie dit (present subjunctive of avoir)	j'aie écrit	j'aie lu	j'aie pris

Irregular verb chart: other irregular verbs, part three

	Partir (sortir, dormir)	Savoir	Voir	Venir (revenir, devenir)
le participe présent present participle	partant leaving	sachant knowing	voyant seeing	venant coming
le présent present tense	je pars tu pars il* part nous partons vous partez ils* partent	je sais tu sais il sait nous savons vous savez ils savent	je vois tu vois il voit nous voyons vous voyez il voient	je viens tu viens il vient nous venons vous venez ils viennent
l'impératif the imperative	dis disons dites	écris écrivons écrivez	lis lisons lisez	prends prenons prenez
l'imparfait imperfect tense	je disais tu disais il disait nous disions vous disiez ils disaient	j'écrivais tu écrivais il écrivait nous écrivions vous écrivions ils écrivaient	je lisais tu lisais il lisait nous lisions vous lisiez ils lisaient	je prenais tu prenais il prenait nous prenions vous preniez ils prenaient
le futur future tense	je dirai tu diras il dira nous dirons vous direz ils diront	j'écrirai tu écriras il écrira nous écrirons vous écrirez ils écriront	je lirai tu liras il lira nous lirons vous lirez ils liront	je prendrai tu prendras il prendra nous prendrons vous prendrez ils prendront
le conditionnel conditional tense	je dirais tu d rais il dirait nous dirions vous diriez ils diraient	j'écrirais tu écrirais il écrirait nous écririons vous écririez ils écriraient	je lirais tu lirais il lirait nous lirions vous liriez ils liraient	je prendrai tu prendrais il prendrai nous prendrions vous prendriez ils prendraient

* il and elle share the same forms just as ils and elles do.

le passé simple simple past tense	je dis tu dis il dit	nous dîmes vous dîtes ils dirent	j'écrivis tu écrivis il écrit	nous écrivîmes vous écrivîtes ils écrivirent	je lus tu lus il lut	nous lûmes vous lûtes ils lurent	je pris tu pris il prit	nous prîmes vous prîtes ils prirent
le subjonctif subjunctive mood	je dise tu dises il dise	nous disions vous disiez ils disent	j'écrive tu écrives il écrive	nous écrivions vous écriviez ils écrivent	je lise tu lises il lise	nous lisions vous lisiez ils lisent	je prenne tu prennes il prenne	nous prenions vous preniez ils prennent

Compound tenses use avoir or être as helping verbs combined with the corresponding past participle.

le passé composé past tense	j'ai dit (present of avoir)	j'ai écrit	j'ai lu	j'ai pris
le plus que parfait pluperfect	j'avais dit (imperfect of avoir)	j'avais écrit	j'avais lu	j'avais pris
le conditionnel passé past conditional	j'aurais dit (conditional of avoir)	j'aurais écrit	j'aurais lu	j'aurais pris
le futur antérieur the future perfect	j'aurai dit (future of avoir)	j'aurai écrit	j'aurai lu	j'aurai pris
le passé du subjonctif past subjunctive	j'aie dit (present subjunctive of avoir)	j'aie écrit	j'aie lu	j'aie pris

INDEX

INDEX

Really. This isn't going to hurt at all . . .

Learning won't hurt when middle school and high school students open any *Painless* title. These books transform subjects into fun—emphasizing a touch of humor and entertaining brain-tickler puzzles that are fun to solve.

Bonus Online Component—each title followed by (*) includes additional online games to challenge students, including Beat the Clock, a line match game, and a word scramble.

Each book: Paperback

Painless Algebra, 4th Ed.*
Lynette Long, Ph.D.
ISBN 978-1-4380-0775-5, $9.99, Can$11.99

Painless American Government
Jeffrey Strausser
ISBN 978-0-7641-2601-7, $9.99, Can$11.99

Painless American History, 2nd Ed.
Curt Lader
ISBN 978-0-7641-4231-4, $9.99, Can$11.99

Painless Chemistry, 2nd Ed.*
Loris Chen
ISBN 978-1-4380-0771-7, $9.99, Can$11.99

Painless Earth Science
Edward J, Denecke, Jr.
ISBN 978-0-7641-4601-5, $9.99, Can$11.99

Painless English for Speakers of Other Languages, 2nd Ed.
Jeffrey Strausser and José Paniza
ISBN 978-1-4380-0002-2, $9.99, Can$11.50

Painless Fractions, 3rd Ed.
Alyece Cummings, M.A.
ISBN 978-1-4380-0000-8, $9.99, Can$11.50

Painless French, 3rd Ed.*
Carol Chaitkin, M.S., and Lynn Gore, M.A.
ISBN 978-1-4380-0770-0, $9.99, Can$11.99

Painless Geometry, 2nd Ed.
Lynette Long, Ph.D.
ISBN 978-0-7641-4230-7, $9.99, Can$11.99

Painless Grammar, 4th Ed.*
Rebecca Elliott, Ph.D.
ISBN 978-1-4380-0774-8, $9.99, Can$11.99

Painless Italian, 2nd Ed.
Marcel Danesi, Ph.D.
ISBN 978-0-7641-4761-6, $9.99, Can$11.50

Painless Math Word Problems, 2nd Ed.
Marcie Abramson, B.S., Ed.M.
ISBN 978-0-7641-4335-9, $9.99, Can$11.99

Painless Poetry, 2nd Ed.
Mary Elizabeth
ISBN 978-0-7641-4591-9, $9.99, Can$11.99

Painless Pre-Algebra, 2nd Ed.*
Amy Stahl
ISBN 978-1-4380-0773-1, $9.99, Can$11.99

Painless Reading Comprehension, 3rd Ed.*
Darolyn "Lyn" Jones, Ed.D.
ISBN 978-1-4380-0769-4, $9.99, Can$11.99

Painless Spanish, 3rd Ed.*
Carlos B. Vega and Dasha Davis
ISBN 978-1-4380-0772-4, $9.99, Can$11.99

Painless Speaking, 2nd Ed.
Mary Elizabeth
ISBN 978-1-4380-0003-9, $9.99, Can$11.50

Painless Spelling, 3rd Ed.
Mary Elizabeth
ISBN 978-0-7641-4713-5, $9.99, Can$11.99

Painless Study Techniques
Michael Greenberg
ISBN 978-0-7641-4059-4, $9.99, Can$11.99

Painless Vocabulary, 3rd Ed.*
Michael Greenberg
ISBN 978-1-4380-0778-6, $9.99, Can$11.99

Painless Writing, 3rd Ed.*
Jeffrey Strausser
ISBN 978-1-4380-0784-7, $9.99, Can$11.99

Prices subject to change without notice.

Available at your local book store or visit **www.barronseduc.com**

(#79) R4/16

Barron's Educational Series, Inc.
250 Wireless Blvd.
Hauppauge, N.Y. 11788
Order toll-free:
1-800-645-3476

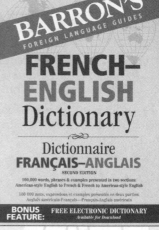